"I'D CHANGE MY LIFE
IF I HAD MORE TIME"

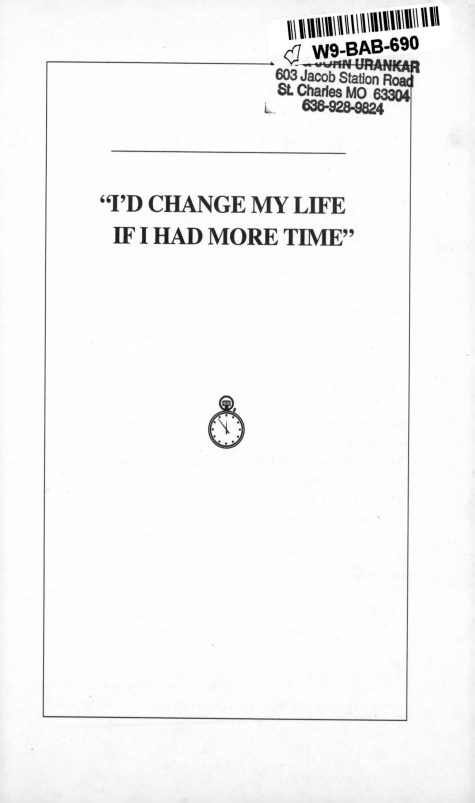

By DOREEN VIRTUE, Ph.D.

Books

THE CHOCOHOLIC'S DREAM DIET
*CONSTANT CRAVING: What Your Food Cravings Mean
    and How to Overcome Them
*"I'D CHANGE MY LIFE IF I HAD MORE TIME":
    A Practical Guide to Making Dreams Come True
IF THIS IS LOVE, WHY AM I LONELY? (by Dr. Helene
    Parker and Doreen Virtue, Ph.D.)
IN THE MOOD
*LOSING YOUR POUNDS OF PAIN: Breaking the Link
    Between Abuse, Stress, and Overeating
MY KIDS DON'T LIVE WITH ME ANYMORE: Coping
    with the Custody Crisis
YO-YO RELATIONSHIPS: How to Beat the I-Need-a-Man
    Habit and Find Stability
THE YO-YO SYNDROME DIET: How to Heal and Stabilize
    Your Appetite and Weight

Audio Book

*LOSING YOUR POUNDS OF PAIN: Breaking the Link
    Between Abuse, Stress, and Overeating

(All of the above are available at your local bookstore. Items marked with an
asterisk [*] may also be ordered by calling Hay House at 800-654-5126.)

"I'D CHANGE MY LIFE IF I HAD MORE TIME"

*A Practical Guide
to Making Dreams Come True*

Doreen Virtue, Ph.D.

Hay House, Inc.
Carlsbad, CA

Copyright © 1996 by Doreen Virtue

Published and distributed in the United States by:
Hay House, Inc.
P.O. Box 5100
Carlsbad, CA 92018-5100
(800) 654-5126

Edited by: Jill Kramer

Designed by: Highpoint, Inc., Claremont, CA

The author of this book does not dispense medical advice or prescribe the use of any technique as a form of treatment for physical or medical problems without the advice of a physician, either directly or indirectly. The intent of the author is only to offer information of a general nature to help you in your quest for emotional well-being and good health. In the event you use any of the information in this book for yourself, which is your constitutional right, the author and the publisher assume no responsibility for your actions.

Library of Congress Cataloging-in-Publication Data

Virtue, Doreen, 1958-
    I'd change my life if I had more time : a practical guide to making dreams come true / by Doreen Virtue.
        p.   cm.
    Includes bibliographical references and index.
    ISBN 1-56170-321-4 (pbk.)
    1. Success—Psychological aspects.   2. Goal (Psychology)   3. Time management.   I. Title.
BF637.S8V553 1996
640.'43—dc20   96-12799
                                                                          CIP

ISBN 1-56170-321-4

99 98 97 96   4 3 2 1
First Printing, August 1996

Printed in the United States of America

To Joan L. Hannan,
my wonderful mother
and truly gifted spiritual healer

and

William C. Hannan,
my fabulous father
and truly gifted author

Thanks, Mom and Dad,
for all your love and gifts!

"To realize the unimportance of time is the gate of wisdom."

— BERTRAND RUSSELL (1872–1970),
NOBEL PEACE PRIZE-WINNING
AUTHOR AND MATHEMATICIAN

C O N T E N T S

PART FOUR: More Time for You!

PART FIVE: Spiritual Support

APPENDIX

P R E F A C E

"The spirit sports with time—can crowd eternity into an hour, or stretch an hour to eternity."

— RALPH WALDO EMERSON (1803–1882),
AMERICAN AUTHOR/PHILOSOPHER

Following the publication of my books, *Constant Craving,* and *Losing Your Pounds of Pain,* many readers said that they were inspired by my ugly-duckling-to-swan transformation story. At one time, I was a fat, uneducated, and extremely unhappy housewife with two small children. I had no income, an unhealthy marriage, and little self-confidence. My only asset was my deep desire to change my life.

I wanted to be a psychologist with a fit body and a harmonious personal life. I also wanted to write self-help books in a house by the beach, but these goals seemed impossible! After all, when would I have time? Besides, the expense of college tuition meant that I'd need a job. Family responsibilities already crammed my schedule; when was I supposed to find time to work, attend college, study, and write? And a beach house? What an expensive dream for someone who could barely make the rent each month! I wanted it all, but not at the expense of my family priorities, or my own peace of mind.

As you'll read, I fulfilled those and other dreams by using the principles outlined in this book. Today, I have a great life filled with love, family, health, purposeful work, relaxation time, and material comforts.

Like many people, I had to reconcile my personal ambitions with my family concerns. I faced worries such as, "Is it selfish to take time away from my family to fulfill my desires?," "If I follow my heart, can I pay my bills?," and "How can I tell my friends that I need to spend my free time working on my goals, instead of talking on the telephone?"

As a lifelong student of religion, philosophy, and metaphysics, I also had spiritual concerns: "What if my will differs from God's will?" "Is it spiritually correct for me to create goals, or should I wait for signs of divine direction?" "Am I spiritually shallow to want material comforts?"

My goals were never to be filthy rich. I wanted financial security, a nice home, and a safe car. I realized that my material needs were secondary to my need to fulfill my spiritual function by being loving and kind. Still, I wanted some reassurance that if I lived a spiritual life, I wouldn't lose sight of down-to-earth concerns such as paying the electricity or phone bill. Couldn't I be a grounded spiritual seeker?

The answer, I found happily, is: "Yes." In fact, spirituality is extremely practical. It's our natural inheritance, a power and sure source of guidance that travels wherever we go. So I know from experience that living a spiritual life does not mean having to endure austere poverty.

On the other hand, worry and obsessions about financial security block one's spiritual progress. It's so important to learn to trust our inner wisdom, and to know that it always leads us to happy rewards. Many people want to simplify their lives, but they worry about how they'll pay the bills while relaxing into their simpler lives. Fortunately, our heart's yearnings direct us toward a meaningful life with a meaningful income. We just need to trust and follow this inner voice.

I learned the hard way that "think and grow rich" doesn't mean merely dreaming about success or early retirement. It means acting upon the inner wisdom we receive. For that reason, in this book, I emphasize the importance of developing and trusting the clear communication you receive from your inner guidance.

My psychological work with survivors of sexual, emotional, and physical abuse has also taught me that childhood traumas can make success a frightening thought. For people raised with messages of "You're not good enough," it's tough to think about embarking on an ambitious life change. (I've written about the link between abuse and overeating in *Losing Your Pounds of Pain*.) In this book, I describe how to overcome the effects of early childhood emotional damage, so you'll *know* you deserve success.

For more than 25 years, I have read hundreds of books and studies on motivation, psychology, metaphysics, philosophy, and sociology. I've also been fortunate to have met and interviewed such great thinkers and authors as Dr. Wayne Dyer, Deepak Chopra, James Redfield, Marianne Williamson, Dr. Robert Schuller, Brian Tracy, Dannion Brinkley (*Saved by the Light*), Betty Eadie (*Embraced by the Light*), Dr. Brian Weiss, and Rosemary Altea (*The Eagle and the Rose*). Here, I've drawn upon a wealth of practical and unique information that will inspire you and guide you to attain your desires—even on a tight schedule.

Unblocking yourself is a worthwhile use of your time and focus, and I've detailed the exact steps that will help you replace fear with confidence, and self-doubt with faith. I've lovingly described just about every step I can think of that will free you from time hindrances, so you'll live more fully. And remember: I'll be with you in spirit every step of the way!

— Doreen Virtue, Ph.D.
Newport Beach, California

ACKNOWLEDGMENTS

I want to thank the women and men who have shared their innermost dreams with me over the years—my clients, workshop attendees, and readers who braved their fears and doubts to change their lives in remarkable ways. You've proven that nothing stands in the way of determination and faith!

I am deeply grateful to Louise L. Hay, Reid Tracy, Jill Kramer, Kristina Queen, Jeannie Liberati, Christy Allison, Ron Tillinghast, Eddie Sandoval, Jenny Richards, and Polly Tracy.

Thank you to my family, friends, and business associates, especially Michael Tienhaara, Charles Schenk, Grant Schenk, Ada Montgomery, Pearl Reynolds, Ted Hannan, Ben Reynolds, Grandma and Grandpa Crane, Lloyd Montgomery, Bonnie Krueger, Martha Carlson, and Allison Bell.

My gratitude also extends to the incredible spiritual leaders I was able to interview and spend time with, including Dr. Wayne Dyer, Marianne Williamson, Deepak Chopra, Betty Eadie, Dannion Brinkley, Dr. Brian Weiss, Dr. Robert Schuller, and Rosemary Altea. What an honor and learning experience to interact with such brilliant minds and loving souls. Thank you!

Finally, a word of deepest thankfulness for the teachers who have inspired me, including Jesus Christ, John Randolph Price, Dr. Kenneth Wapnick, Catherine Ponder, Emmet Fox, Ernest Holmes, Mary Baker Eddy, Dr. Norman Vincent Peale, Dr. Napoleon Hill, Ruth Montgomery, and Forrest Holly.

BREAKING THE TIME-CRUNCH CYCLE

"For of all sad words of tongue or pen, the saddest are these: 'It might have been!'"
— JOHN GREENLEAF WHITTIER (1807–1892),
AMERICAN POET

+ *"I wish I had more time. I'd start my own business so I could work from home."*
+ *"I'd love to exercise, but my kids and job take every moment of the day!"*
+ *"Someday, I'll get around to taking that night class, but right now my schedule's too tight."*
+ *"I'll get started on my goals just as soon as the kids finish school, and the weddings, visitors, vacations, and holidays are out of the way."*

No More Pushing

Do you want more time to fulfill your dreams and desires? Are most of your hours devoted to duties, leaving little time for relaxation, self-improvement, or family? Do you push yourself past the point of exhaustion while taking care of everyone else's needs? Do you wish someone would help you with housework so you'd have more time to enjoy yourself? Do you need more time and money to switch to a more rewarding career or lifestyle?

If so, then this book is for you. As a full-time working mother of two teenagers, I wish *I'd* had access to this book many years ago! I've read many books and attended lots of seminars on time management, only to find much of the advice offered there unrealistic or just plain silly. Instead, I learned firsthand how to enjoy my family, career, college, fitness, meditation, and moments alone. I wrote this book to share these effective and realistic solutions to time crunches—solutions that *subtract* from your stress levels, rather than *add* to them.

Here you'll find guidance and courage to create a joyful, meaningful, and prosperous life. And you'll also discover step-by-step methods for accessing inner and spiritual guidance so you'll feel sure about the direction in which you are headed.

But first, let me ask you some important questions:

1. How would your life improve if you had more unstructured time?
2. What changes would you make?
3. How would your relationships change?
4. How would you spend your extra time?

If you can imagine how your life would improve by having more time, you're on your way toward realizing that desire. You can do it!

Off the Fast Track

You probably know that you're not alone in wanting a simpler, more meaningful life. Dozens of recent surveys show that we're tired of chasing the dollar while sacrificing our families and home life. Here's what researchers have discovered:

+ *We're rushed.* Thirty-eight percent of us "always feel rushed," according to a 1992 National Parks and Recreation Association survey. More women than men (37 versus 32 percent) and more marrieds than singles (41 versus 33 percent) claim that this is the case much of the time.

✦ *We're stressed.* Seventy percent of us experience stress on a weekly basis, and 30 percent claim to be under "a lot of stress," according to a 1995 *U.S. News and World Report*/Bozell survey.

✦ *We crave relaxation more than money.*

— Sixty-six percent of men and women in a 1993 Roper survey of 1,000 adult Americans said that "making lots of money isn't as important to me as it was five years ago."

— Fifty-one percent of Americans want more time for themselves, even if it means earning less money, according to the 1995 *U.S. News and World Report*/Bozell survey.

— Thirty-three percent of Americans are willing to take a 20 percent cut in pay in exchange for a shorter work week, according to a 1993 Gallup poll.

— In the last 10 years, 21 percent of DuPont employees have turned down promotions that would mean more job pressure, and 24 percent have passed up promotions that would require travel. A 1992 survey of 8,500 DuPont employees found that 57 percent of men want flex time so they can be at home with their families more often.

✦ *We have shifted priorities.*

— A 1995 Merck Family Fund poll found that 45 percent of mothers have voluntarily reduced both employment and earnings, along with 32 percent of childless women and 23.5 percent of all men.

— Eighty-seven percent of women and 72 percent of men surveyed in the Merck poll said they want to spend more time caring for their children.

— Sixty-three percent of working women and 54 percent of working men said their view of success had changed, according to a 1993 Roper poll conducted for *Working Woman* magazine.

— Sixty-six percent of people surveyed by the Harwood Group in 1995 said they would be more satisfied with their lives if they were able to spend more time with family and friends. Only 15 percent in the same survey said that having nicer things in their home would lead to greater life satisfaction.

✦ *Our health is affected.* The 1995 *U.S. News and World Report*/Bozell survey also discovered these worrisome trends:

— Forty-three percent of us currently suffer from physical and psychological burnout symptoms.

— About 75 to 90 percent of our health-care visits are directly related to this stress and burnout.

✦ *Moms have less free time.* Women have less leisure time than men, especially women between the ages of 35 and 44 with children under 15 years of age. (Source: *Leisure Intelligence Journal*, 1995.)

✦ *Simplicity equals happiness.* Eighty-six percent of people surveyed by the Harwood Group in 1995, who had voluntarily downshifted their working hours, said that they were happy with the changes, reported *The New York Times*. Only 9 percent of the voluntary downshifters stated that they were unhappy with their new lifestyle.

Millennium Shift

These trends clearly point in the same direction: our fast-paced, materialistic frenzy of past decades didn't give us the health and happiness we expected. We're now willing to trade in overtime pay for a few moments alone with ourselves and our loved ones. Still, many people feel stuck in overstressed lifestyles. They worry about losing their jobs and employee benefits if they refuse to work overtime or travel on company business. "Sure, I'd love to simplify my life, but my kids still need health insurance and a roof over their heads," these folks legitimately retort.

Fortunately, there are ways to ensure that your material and psychological needs are simultaneously met, as you'll read throughout this book.

ARE YOU SUFFERING FROM A TIME CRUNCH?

Many people tell me that they dream of a more fulfilling life, but responsibilities keep them locked in a too-tight schedule. The cruel irony is that they don't feel that they have time to change their lives!

Researchers studying this time-crunch phenomenon posed the following questions to 1,010 Americans. See how your answers compare, by responding to each statement with a "true"or "false."

Statement:	% Answering "True":	Your Answer:
1. I often feel under stress when I don't have enough time.	43	_____
2. When I need more time, I tend to cut back on my sleep.	40	_____

Statement:	% Answering "True":	Your Answer:
3. At the end of the day, I often feel that I haven't accomplished what I set out to do.	33	_____
4. I worry that I don't spend enough time with my family or friends.	33	_____
5. I feel that I'm constantly under stress—trying to accomplish more than I can handle.	31	_____
6. I feel trapped in a daily routine.	28	_____
7. When I'm working long hours, I often feel guilty that I'm not at home.	27	_____
8. I consider myself a workaholic.	26	_____
9. I just don't have time for fun.	22	_____
10. Sometimes I feel that my spouse doesn't know who I am anymore.	21	_____

Interpreting your results: If you responded "true" to three or more statements, you are suffering from a time crunch.

In the national survey, women averaged 3.5 "true" answers, while men answered "true" to approximately 2.9 questions. Those most likely to experience a time crunch were divorced or widowed females, ages 18 to 49, with full-time jobs and children at home between 6 and 17 years of age. (Source: Hilton Time Survey, 1991.)

Priceless Love

We've reshuffled our priorities, and money is no longer our prime incentive for getting up every morning. Fortunately, a new study finds that we may not have to sacrifice financial security to spend more time with our families. In fact, the opposite may be true! A 1995 Wharton School study compared the earnings of those whose top priority was money with those whose top priority was family. The researchers discovered that people who placed great importance on finding a compatible spouse and enjoying a good family life actually *made more money* than people who put finances before family!

Perhaps emotionally fulfilled people perform and concentrate better at work. Their office social skills might reflect their people priorities, making them naturally warm and caring co-workers. In other words, they are well liked by themselves, their family, and their employers.

The Wharton School study underscores how reshuffling priorities can give us more of what we want: time with our families, plus a healthy income. Here are the results of a recent national survey that asked Americans to rank their current top three priorities. How does this list compare with your own?

WHAT ARE YOUR PRIORITIES?

Issue:	% Who Rank It As a "Top 3 Priority"*
1. Family life	68
2. Spiritual life	46
3. Health	44
4. Finances	25
5. Careers	23
6. Romantic life	18
7. Leisure activities	14
8. House and home	11

Source: Bozell / KRC Research, *U.S. News & World Report*, December 1995

*Percentages exceed 100% because respondents gave three answers

A Brief Shuffle

Reorganization of anything—a closet, a corporation, or our own lives—necessarily creates turmoil and unrest before things settle back into a smooth operation. When I clean out my closets in the spring, the house initially looks messier as I move clothes and boxes onto the floor. Anyone walking into my house during my closet-cleaning session would assume a cyclone had just gone through! Yet, the mess is worth it once the closet is straightened and organized.

I guess you can see my point: as you reshuffle your schedule to accommodate new priorities and activities, it may initially feel as though your life gets messier. But hang in there, because—as with my closet—you'll soon see a smooth pattern of progress emerging.

Do
Less,
Have
More

FREE TIME...AT NO COST

"There is more to life than just increasing its speed."
— MAHATMA GANDHI (1869–1948), INDIAN
NATIONALIST AND SPIRITUAL LEADER

Time is an odd phenomenon. It's one of the most abundant and renewable resources we have. It's also free of charge. Yet, we often feel like "time paupers." Every day we receive 24 hours, at no cost. It doesn't matter who you are, what sex, race, or religion. Every morning we wake up with ownership of all the hours in the day. If you live to be 86 years old, you'll have more than 750,000 hours to use any way you want.

So why do we feel an intense anxiety and pressure about time? Why do we feel tense, angry, ripped off, or depressed when we allocate our time in unsatisfying ways? Why do we feel as if family, friends, co-workers, or employers demand control over our time?

Part of the problem is that each year we live becomes a progressively smaller piece of the lifespan pie. When you were five, a year was one-fifth of your entire life, so it seemed like an eternity before your sixth birthday. Yet when you are 30, one year is a much smaller 1/30th of your lifespan. When you are 40, a year is an even smaller 1/40th pie piece, and so on. Each year goes by faster because it is a smaller percentage of your life.

As we pile on ever more responsibilities, debts, chores, and obligations, we divvy up the daily moments into smaller and smaller bits. We disperse our attention in so many directions that the day zips by. If the duties we're attending to aren't personally exciting or meaningful, we fantasize about some future day when things will be better. By not living in the moment, in the here-and-now, we remove ourselves from fully experiencing the day. Like driving a car while daydreaming, you arrive at the end of the day without knowing how you got there.

Fear and worry deplete energy, which further shrinks our productive time, and money can be a major factor in creating those emotions. As companies reduce the size of their workforce, many people find themselves doing the job of three, while simultaneously looking over their shoulders for an impending pink slip. The people I talk with across the country are terrified of financial lack. They crave comfort, meaning, and security. Perhaps you feel the same way.

"Lack mentality" directed toward time is a self-fulfilling prophecy. Constant worries and fears concerning lack of time are energy draining and creativity blocking! Remind yourself often, "There is plenty of time!" Say it over and over again, and your tension *will* dissipate. Our schedules feel freer once we release the concern that there isn't enough time.

Creating Spare Time

Responsibilities can make us feel locked into claustrophobic schedules. Still, there are methods for breaking free! First, I want to emphasize the value of investing little chunks of spare time in goal fulfillment. Ten minutes here, thirty minutes there—these moments add up substantially, like pennies in a piggy bank.

I'm not suggesting that you stuff more activities into an overstuffed schedule. What I'm suggesting throughout this book are ways to use time for optimum physical, mental, emotional, spiritual, and financial health. This health doesn't come from pushing against life, but relaxing into it. Resentment and anger over tight schedules does nothing but rob us of the peace, enjoyment, and financial security we want and deserve.

My psychotherapy and teaching work with thousands of men and women over the past decade has convinced me that three factors interfere with achieving these desires:

1. Fear
2. Disorganized schedules
3. Not using the awesome spiritual power available to all of us. This power is unlimited, and miraculously and instantaneously heals financial, career, health, family, and love-life problems. (We'll discuss all three factors throughout this book.)

Whatever it is that you're dreaming of—relaxation, playtime with the kids, finishing your degree, opening a business, writing a book, exercising, or meditating—you needn't wait for the future, thinking that's when you'll have extra time. Spare time happens *now*, through conscious choices and decisions. For example, in the time it takes to watch a mindless television program, read the newspaper cover-to-cover, or have a long telephone chat, we could accomplish one step toward fulfilling a dream. The thrill of accomplishing that one step is enough to fuel the energy you need to fulfill your other obligations.

> *Remember: we don't **find** spare time; we **create** it.*

Where Does the Time Go?

These sentiments are at the heart of most complaints I hear about not having enough time:

✦ "I feel guilty or selfish taking time for myself."

✦ "I don't feel prepared to begin working on my personal desires."
✦ "I don't have the self-discipline to set, and stick to, a schedule for the accomplishment of my goals."
✦ "I'm not really clear about what I want. I just know I'm unhappy about the way my life currently is."
✦ "I'm afraid that if I put time into my desires, my income will drop, with serious consequences."

I understand these fears and hesitations, because I've held on to them myself. Then I discovered how much energy I was wasting by having little mental arguments with myself. For instance, I'd think: I should go to the gym today. Then I'd think: But I haven't spent enough time with my kids this week. On and on, I'd argue with myself.

"Enough!" I finally told myself. "There has got to be another way!" There was. First, I learned how to take small steps toward accomplishing big goals. It's the old write-one-page-a-day-and-you'll-have-a-book-in-one-year approach, and it really is true. Second, I looked for ways to complete these small steps in the spare five or ten minutes waiting in line at the bank, on hold on the telephone, or watching television with my family.

And speaking of watching television:

> Q: What do you suppose is the number-one daily activity that Americans engage in during their free time?
>
> A: Television viewing!

We spend 30 percent of all free time in front of the television set, according to a study conducted by Leisure Trends between 1990 and 1992 and reported in *American Demographics* magazine.

Eighty-four percent of us watch television at least three hours a week, according to a 1994 study of the President's Council on Physical Fitness. Families with children spend even more time watching television—6.3 hours a week, according to a 1994 Angus Reid poll.

If you were tightening your money budget, you'd first trim the nonessentials. It's no different with time. Since television viewing is a major time drain, there are at least four options to consider:

1. *Go ahead and enjoy watching television.* It *is* a relaxing and relatively inexpensive activity, after all! Instead of feeling guilty (guilt drains energy and enthusiasm) because you're curled up in front of the TV, give yourself permission to enjoy it. Television viewing is even more pleasurable when cuddling with a loved one, or by sharing and discussing a program with your children. You can have a picnic on the floor in front of the television, or enjoy popcorn and soda while sharing some laughs.

2. *Work on projects while watching television.* Why not capitalize on the time? It's possible to ride a stationary bicycle, write thank-you letters, read the newspaper, or work on your major goal while sitting in front of the TV. I've done this type of doubling-up for years, and it's a great way to have my cake and eat it, too!

3. *Be selective.* Videotape and watch only your favorite shows and specials. Fast-forward through commercials. Avoid aimlessly sitting in front of the television, surfing through the channels in the hopes of finding anything that's remotely entertaining. Have designated "television hours," instead of treating your living room as a 24-hour, 7-day-a-week movie theater.

4. *Pull the plug.* Avoid watching television for seven days, and notice what happens to your schedule. You'll probably find

that you and your family read and talk more often. You'll have more time to devote to things that really matter to you, and you may decide to permanently replace the television with an aquarium or a bookshelf.

Television viewing isn't inherently bad. But for many of us, it's a logical starting point in our quest for more time.

How We Spend Our Weekends

Another source of free time are those glorious weekend days which, for most of us, extend from Friday to Sunday night. But did you ever promise yourself that you'd work on your goals on the weekend when you had more time? Then Sunday night comes, and you wonder what happened to those golden opportunities. Most weekends are spent on chores, according to one national survey. Here's how those hours break down:

Activity	Time spent per weekend
Working at your job	2 hours, 54 minutes
Cooking	2 hours
Cleaning	2 hours, 17 minutes
Running errands	1 hour, 43 minutes
Doing laundry	1 hour, 18 minutes
Making household repairs	1 hour, 12 minutes
Grocery shopping	59 minutes
Paying bills	34 minutes

Source: Hilton Time Survey, 1991.

Looking at this list, it's no wonder we're craving fun and a simpler lifestyle! How many of these activities could be streamlined, delegated, or eliminated? We'll look at ways to capitalize upon these precious moments throughout this book.

Focused Time

Studies show that given a choice to perform a difficult-but-desired activity OR a simple-but-less-desired activity, most of us will opt for the second option because it's easier. The only way we'll work on a more difficult task is if we're excited about it.

In this book, I'll help to fire up your excitement about your goals by showing you:

+ how to pinpoint exactly what life changes you want;
+ how to fire up your determination to succeed;
+ how to find the greatest help and direction from your inner guide;
+ ways to accomplish your goals on a tight schedule;
+ how to reclaim ownership of your free time and work time; and
+ how to identify and overcome fear, guilt, and self-doubts that keep you from starting or completing your goals.

Many of my well-meaning clients, friends, and acquaintances have told me of plans to change their lives when they get more time. An acquaintance of mine named Lorraine enthusiastically told me of her dream to write a mystery novel. She'd taken many writing courses, and had a plot, characters, and all the basic workings of the book.

"I'm so excited about this book!" Lorraine said, "I'll start writing it during my summer vacation."

When I saw Lorraine in the fall, I asked how her book was going. Her enthusiasm for the project hadn't dampened; however, she explained that her vacation had *flown* by. "I just didn't get enough time to start writing!" she complained.

I do not judge Lorraine's behavior in any way. I know, from first-hand experience, that starting a valued project is difficult. I know how painful it is to face the fear of failure. How much simpler it is to keep *preparing* to fulfill your dream, rather than actually doing it. It's procrastination based on the thought, "I'm almost ready, but not quite yet."

I've also had to overcome fears that paralyzed me into chronic paralysis. I've broken my impasse by asking myself, "What's the worst thing that could happen to me if I go for it?" Usually, the answer is embarrassment or experiencing a painful rejection. Then I ask myself, "What's the worst thing that could happen to me if I DON'T go for it?" This second answer is usually more painful to think about than the first. Finally, I turn my thoughts to happier images of the BEST things that will happen to me as a result of going for it. Those pleasant mental images usually spur me into action.

Many people are busy with activities that they neither want nor enjoy. Every day, I hear from clients and readers who say that they are frightened by lack in their lives—lack of money, love, and health. They are frustrated because they're so busy, yet so lacking in what they really want. What kind of life is that?

If you are tired of pushing without reward, remember that *pushing is the whole problem*. Like those little Chinese finger tubes, the harder we push and pull, the more life constricts. When we are frantically busy and afraid, we don't listen to the inner guide desperately seeking our attention. This inner guide, as you'll later read, is your personalized interactive source for the greatest financial, emotional, and health wisdom around. You'll fall in love with this combination counselor and best friend who is always with you!

Without Fear, All Is Possible

I was a young mother of two active little boys when I first decided to write a book. I had recently gone back to work as an insurance company secretary, and was attending college part-time.

Out of necessity, I quickly learned the value of short chunks of time. In one half-hour, you can accomplish quite a bit if you put your mind to it! With all the goals and responsibilities I had, there was no time to waste on television, or lengthy telephone chats with girlfriends. I realized I had to make definite choices about how to spend my time if I was going to accomplish anything.

First, I created a list of my short- and long-term priorities. My spirituality, my family, my emotional and physical health, my education, and writing were my focus. I cut out time-consuming nonessentials, such as going to movies, attending parties, and going out to dinner. Like cutting the fat out of a diet, I was streamlining my schedule.

You'd think that all this intense planning and prioritizing would have turned me into a stressed-out person. Just the opposite occurred! The more I fulfilled my priorities, the better I felt about myself, my family, and my life. My stress level actually decreased! Very soon, my friends were asking to know about my "secret" to getting things done.

Stretching an Hour

I believe that the only reason I accomplished my dream was the depth of my burning desire. Inside was this NEED to write; that's the only way to describe it. In fact, I had a terrifying fear that I'd die before I had a chance to write my first book. Fame and fortune weren't my motivators (although I don't discount those perks of publication). It was a need to leave a mark on the world, some evidence I'd been here. Posterity, immortality—those were the goals of my soul.

My writing sessions were like the movie cliché of a housewife typing her book at the kitchen table late at night when the kids are asleep. It was the only time I had! This was before personal computers, so I'd first handwrite my thoughts and then type them, correcting any errors with liquid correction fluid.

My commitment to goals and priorities was not without struggle! When I was first writing, I developed a sudden and consuming interest in picking out lint between the carpet yarns. Seriously! I also became preoccupied with cleaning dust out from under the refrigerator. I thought, "You can't begin writing until the house is perfectly clean." Looking back, I realize that my procrastination was protection against the possibility of failure. After all, what if I couldn't find a publisher for my book? Rather than face that disappointment, it would be easier to not even try!

I also struggled with writer's block. Every time I'd sit at the typewriter, I'd get real antsy inside and decide to clean the house instead of write. After a week of this, I asked my psychology professor for some advice. Her words still ring in my ears: "Just write!" There was my answer, plain and simple: *Just do it.*

So I bought a calendar and set down a writing schedule, in ink. I stuck to that schedule and happily crossed off each day on the calendar. Within three weeks, I had completed a book proposal. Eight months later, I had a book contract in my hands!

Taking a Time Inventory

If you are frustrated because your life seems to be on hold, you are not alone! So many bright, successful people over the years have told me about their thwarted intentions, about feeling stuck in the mud of responsibilities with their wheels spinning around and around.

As I stated earlier, my intent with this guidebook is to help you lose the energy-draining and time-consuming fat from your schedule. Again, I'm not advising you to become a superwoman or a superman! Part of your life change may involve simplifying your life and having fewer activities, responsibilities, and possessions.

The point is to create the kind of life that best suits *you.* To do this, I'm proposing five steps:

1. Form a clear picture of what you want (which could include more free and leisure time).

2. Identify, eliminate, or reduce fears, beliefs, or doubts that block you.
3. Get rid of the time-wasters and energy-drainers from your life.
4. Strengthen your intuitive and spiritual communication skills so you'll know *how* to fulfill your goals.
5. Use short chunks of time to make steady progress toward these desires.

POINTS TO REMEMBER

ૐ We don't find spare time. We must create it.

ૐ It's important to use little chunks of time toward the fulfillment of our desires, instead of waiting for some future day when we'll have "more time."

ૐ Being busy doesn't equate to being truly productive. Question each activity to see if it is really necessary, or if it's merely a product of fear or guilt.

ૐ Pushing against time reinforces the illusion of lack. It's vital to flow with time, not fight against it. This calmer approach helps us to hear our inner guide's advice about health, love, spirituality, and money.

In the next chapter, we'll look at the powerful effect your decisions and beliefs about time have upon making your dreams come true. Keep going—the best is yet to come!

ૐ   ૐ   ૐ

THE GOALS OF YOUR SOUL

"If you keep calm, with intense concentration, you will perform all duties with the correct speed."

— PARAMAHANSA YOGANANDA (1893–1952),
AUTHOR OF *AUTOBIOGRAPHY OF A YOGI,*
AND FOUNDER OF THE SELF-REALIZATION
FELLOWSHIP

Imagine yourself 70 or 80 years from now. You have passed on to the other side. You look upon the earth and see people much like you were: struggling, competing, and worried. Yet you clearly see that each of these people has hopes and dreams. You also have learned, since your transition following physical death, that they could have anything they want through focused intent.

You understand that people can change their lives by making a firm decision. You also see how you missed so many opportunities while on earth. "I could have been, had, or done anything I wanted," you wistfully recall. "If only I'd had enough faith in myself and other people, my life would have been so different!"

While looking upon this scene, you recognize someone that you knew and loved while on the earthplane. You see this person struggling to get ahead, and recognize this as your opportunity to help. So you intervene and create a miraculous coincidence that will bring this person closer to her goals. Unfortunately, your earth-

bound friend pushes this opportunity away because she doesn't believe that it's yet time to collect her good fortune.

She doesn't realize that she—like all of us—*deserves* success.

You DO Deserve Success

So many of my clients have talked to me about their dreams,
hopes, and aspirations. Although they aspired to improve their lives,
they felt blocked for many reasons. Usually they vocalized these
blocks in the complaint, *"I'd change my life if I had more time!"*

Suzanne, a real estate office secretary, admitted her secret dream to me in therapy one day: she'd always
yearned to write children's books. The only trouble
was, after working an eight-hour day and taking care of
her children and housework, Suzanne had little time or energy left over.

Another client, Corinne, said she'd like nothing more
than to get married and start a family. But her busy schedule, which includes a management job, night school, and
aerobic workouts, left her little time or energy to find and
date suitable men.

Mark, a 37-year-old civil engineer, has always wanted
to earn his small aircraft pilot's license. He keeps waiting
for a time when his schedule will give him the breathing
room for flying lessons.

Robin wants to lose weight and get her body in shape,
but she wonders when she'll have the time to exercise.
She devotes her mornings to getting her kids ready for
school, and her daytime job as a nurse affords no break
times. At night, Robin has to prepare dinner and help her

children with homework. With such a tight schedule, when was she supposed to fit in a workout?

LuAnne dreams of quitting her stuffy old job to open a consulting business. She realizes that self-employment requires complete devotion and focus. LuAnne wonders how she can fulfill her present job responsibilities and start a new business simultaneously. "I can't afford to quit my job until my new business becomes profitable," she explains. "But the catch-22 is that I can't make a new business profitable while working at another job full-time!"

Many of my clients took out their frustrations on themselves through self-abusive behavior such as overeating. I've written about the use of food for comfort in my books, *Losing Your Pounds of Pain*, and *Constant Craving*. My therapeutic stance has always been that if you focus on improving your life, your appetite will normalize, and weight loss naturally follows. Because of this philosophy—my specialty has been the treatment of compulsive overeaters—I've always incorporated family, marriage, career, and spiritual counseling to evoke healing.

Consequently, after 12 years of counseling thousands of women and men, I've identified clear patterns in people who feel thwarted from reaching their goals. My successes in helping others move toward achieving their dreams have inspired me to write this guidebook for you. Whatever your heart's desire, know that you can achieve it through the process of unblocking your fears and self-doubts.

"I Could've Done That!"

How often have you seen a book, piece of artwork, or other accomplishment and said to yourself, "I could have done that!" or "Why didn't I think of doing something like that?!" How often have you seen a loving couple in a restaurant or park and sighed,

"Why can't I have a wonderful romantic relationship?" Similarly, how often have you noticed a trim-figured healthy person and wished you had a body just like his or hers?

Making yourself miserable by envying other people's lives doesn't bring you any closer to realizing these aspirations. Jealousy of other people's accomplishments literally slams the door to your success, because it negatively affirms that there's not enough good to go around. Jealousy assumes that if one person wins, the other necessarily loses—in other words, one lacks. When you affirm you are a loser or that you are lacking, guess what manifests in your life? Loss of some kind!

Some people are motivated by fear—fear of poverty, fear of losing their partner's love, or fear of gaining weight, for instance. Fear is an ineffective motivator because it results in poor decision making and low creativity. Other people sense your fears and insecurities, and they are repelled, as opposed to being inspired to help you. There is no power or magic in fear, but there's *unlimited* power and magic in fear's opposite: love and joy.

With success, then, attitude and beliefs are everything. In fact, it's safe to say that getting ahead doesn't depend so much on who you know, but *how* you know. Even during the darkest moments of financial insecurity, relationship troubles, and health or weight concerns, you can still choose which type of thought to hold:

> *A fear-based thought that focuses on the apparent problems of the situation*
>
> *OR*
>
> *A love-based thought that focuses on the possibilities and directs the situation toward a happy outcome.*

Here are some examples of "fear-full" thoughts that block the fruition of desires. If you are frustrated about any part of your life, see if a fear-based thought is behind it. If so, the chart gives some "power-full" alternative thoughts. Write or read the positive thoughts twice a day for 30 days, and you'll form a mental habit that demands positive action and creates desirable results.

CHANGE FEAR THOUGHTS INTO LOVE-POWERED THOUGHTS

Fear-Based Thoughts

Love-Based Thoughts

1. "I'm afraid I'll run out of money and be destitute."

"I work hard and am responsible with my money. I'm doing my part, and I trust God to do His part in taking care of me as well."

2. "All the good single people are taken. I'll never be in a good relationship, and will be alone for the rest of my life."

"I know that my wonderful mate is looking for me as much as I am seeking him (or her). I relax and trust the spiritual world to act as intermediaries in bringing us together naturally, in the right time and place."

3. "I'd better hurry to get ahead in my career."

"I pay attention to my intuition and follow its direction. I trust that all my needs will be met."

4. "Other people always interfere with my plans. If I could just get away by myself, everything would be different."

"I take responsibility for every situation in my life, and now decide to attract positive and supportive people who will support my dreams."

5. "What if I get fired and I can't pay my bills? What if I lose my house or car?"

"I take good care of myself and my responsibilities today. I trust that all my tomorrows will be taken care of in the same manner."

6. "Bad things always seem to happen to me. I need to stay on guard to foresee any impending disasters."

"I take necessary precautions, and visualize good things happening to me (I know that I can create a bad situation just by focusing on it)."

Fear-Based Thoughts	Love-Based Thoughts
7. "I feel insecure, as if I'm one day away from losing everything."	"I am secure, knowing that my thoughts and efforts are directed in positive directions. Whatever comes up, I know I'll be able to handle it."
8. "There's never enough time for anything!"	"There's enough time for me to address all of my needs."
9. "I'm afraid that if I don't exercise every day, I'll gain weight."	"Exercise gives me high energy, and makes me feel alive. I know that if I miss a day of exercise, I'll still be healthy and fit."
10. "Everyone's always trying to get the best of me."	"I expect the best from all those around me, and I get it!"

Reach for the Stars

There are no limits to the changes you can make in your life. All that is required is to firmly decide that you want—and expect—the change. The key word is *firm*, because lukewarm decisions create lukewarm results. Telling yourself, "I *guess* I'd like a new house someday..." won't stimulate yourself or the universe into action. Lukewarm statements like this belie the thoughts behind them, such as: "I'd like to change my life, but I don't really expect it to happen."

But a firm decision—now that's a whole different story! When you put your foot down and declare, "This is what I will and won't accept in my life," the universe gives you a standing ovation. It then delivers exactly what you ordered—sometimes immediately.

Everything in our life is a projection of our thoughts, like images beaming out from a film projector. Change your thoughts, and you've essentially changed the film in the projector. Conversely, the image that shines out also changes. As *A Course in Miracles* says, "All appearances can change *because* they are appearances."

The Appearance of Time

If we believe it takes a long time to get a new job, a different house, or a better relationship, it *will* take a long time. But when we believe it's possible for changes to instantly occur, then they do! The nice thing about your dreams is that, since you are the dreamer, you get to decide on all the details. You can even pinpoint how long your dreams will take to manifest into tangible form.

I've always rejected conventional notions about how much time goals are "supposed" to take. I guess I don't like rules that much. Either that, or I'm impatient (I could make a joke right here about patience being a virtue, but *this* Virtue isn't patient). I've had people tell me how much time things would take, and instead of believing them, I vow to prove their time rules wrong.

For example, a college professor told my first-year psychology class that we'd have to wait until we received advanced degrees before we could work in the field. I got a counseling job at a major psychiatric hospital four months later. Another college professor, upon hearing my goal to become published, said I couldn't write a book until I'd received my doctorate. My first book was published several years before I became a Ph.D.

These are just a few examples, albeit defiant ones, of how I've refused to abide by traditional measures of time. Many of my friends and clients who share my convictions tell similar stories. The bottom line is this:

> *Whatever you believe about time—that you have plenty, or that you don't have enough—you are correct!*

Demand Your Dreams!

After conquering limiting beliefs about time, it's important to fully expect your dreams to be realized. It's not enough to hope that your life will change; you must *expect* it!

So…

> Don't just *wish* for your dreams to come true,
> but passionately *want* them!
>
> Don't just *hope* for your dreams,
> but *know* they are coming to you right this minute!
>
> Don't *fear* that good things only happen to other people,
> but *know* that good is for everyone, including you!
>
> Don't just *request* that your divine path come true.
> Put your foot down and *demand* it!

Think about any situation in your past where you've put your foot down. Perhaps your child or pet needed emergency medical care, your romantic partner mistreated you, or someone tried to sell you shoddy goods. Remember how black and white your thinking was at that moment? There was no way you would accept any alternative to what you wanted!

Now, transfer that passionate determination to your goals.

Manifesting, Here and Now

Sheer determination helped me manifest a new home for myself. As I said before, you can instantly change your life if you truly believe it is possible. Goals only take a lot of time to manifest when we place human expectations about time and conditions on them.

A few years ago, I was living in a small rented apartment next to a tiny river. I'm a real water baby, someone who virtually *needs* to live next to a body of water. The sight of a lake, ocean, or river makes my soul sing and my creativity soar. However, the little river next to my apartment was narrow and hidden by brush. I could sort of hear the water babble over rocks, but couldn't really see the water from my window. I was unhappy with my disappointing view, and even unhappier with the fact that I was renting instead of owning.

One day, I woke up in one of those mean and nasty moods. I was sick of the whole situation! Sick of my cramped quarters. Sick of throwing money away on rent. And mostly sick of not being able to see water from my window. That day, I vowed to move—no ifs, ands, or buts—this girl had made up her mind!

I knew what kind of place I wanted to move into. I gave my imagination full rein to imagine all the details I desired, much like a computer forming one unified image from a composite of pictures. I visualized a dream home, yet my dream-home image was one that my mind could accept as a believable goal. I didn't visualize buying a mansion, since at that time I wouldn't have imagined it was possible. And without belief, dreams don't manifest into tangible reality.

I knew my home would have a waterfront location. I could picture myself living in a moderate-sized condominium on the shores of a nearby lake. Nothing too fancy, just cute and in good condition. I would own this place, and firmly decided to pay less per month than my current rent rate. Oh, yes, one more thing: since I hadn't saved much money, I wanted to buy it with no money down.

Looking back, it's interesting that I never even questioned the validity of my desire. I knew what I wanted, and that was that! I put my foot down that morning. My decision process was no different from asking a waitress to replace a dirty glass with a clean one, or expecting a department store to refund an overcharge.

The Obedient Inner Guide

Once you put your order in, the universe promptly delivers it. However, your new house, job, outlook, career, or love partner won't just plop into your lap. The doorbell won't just ring, with a barrel of money sitting there on your doorstep.

Instead, you'll get subtle nudges (what I also call "gut feelings," "an inner guide," "hunches" or "intuition") that instruct you to take some action. You might get a hunch to call a certain person, read a specific book, take a particular class, or drive to a certain business. Believe me, these instructions are the answers to your prayers. Follow them obediently, and you'll see your dreams literally manifest in front of your eyes—sometimes piece by piece, sometimes immediately.

We form a team with our inner guide. It wants us to fulfill our life purpose, so it nags at us when we stray from our path. In response to the inner guide's urges to change our life, we create new mental images of how our life should be. The inner guide responds to our mental images as obediently as a faithful servant. Then we, in turn, must obey its guidance to manifest our dream's fruition. *Always* follow your intuition, even if it seems outlandish or silly.

My intuition guided me to the home of my dreams. That very morning when I'd decided to change residences, I was driving to work when a strong hunch prompted me to turn onto a little side street. I obeyed the instinct, and found myself on a winding road near the lake I loved so much.

My inner guide pulled at me like a seeing-eye dog, and I followed it—although I must admit I wondered what the heck I was doing on this side road when I was already late for work. Then, my eyes caught a sight that confirmed that my gut instincts were correct: there in front of me was a gorgeous Cape Cod-style two-story condominium with bay windows overlooking the lake. Its most beautiful feature was the large "For Sale" sign perched on a geranium-clad window sill.

My hands shook as I copied down the Realtor's telephone number, because I knew—*I just knew*—that this was my future home! I could barely drive to work, I was so excited to call the number on the "For Sale" sign. As soon as I got to my office, everything clicked: I was immediately able to speak with the sales agent. He agreed to meet me at the condo that afternoon.

The inside of the condo was even cuter than its outside, although it definitely needed some TLC and a good cleaning to spruce it up. The price of the condo was a fraction of what I'd expected. As far as I was concerned, the place was already mine! I explained my financial needs to the sales agent who, it turned out, owned the condominium. He agreed to my no-money-down terms, and one hour later I had a signed contract and a key in my hand. That weekend, I moved into the condominium that I had only dreamed about a short while ago.

Purrrfectly Content

Wait, there's more! Naturally, I needed a cat to go with my new home. I had a clear picture of what my dream cat would be like (by this time, my confidence in manifesting was at an all-time high!). I imagined a beautiful long-haired Himalayan with big blue eyes. I wanted an adult cat who had been neutered and who had its shots. One more thing: as with my condo, I wanted the cat to be free of charge.

BOOM! I had made another firm decision, and my gut instincts got to work once again. I was guided to open the yellow pages to the "Veterinarians" section. One particular veterinarian's ad jumped out at me. I dialed his number, again on intuition.

I told the receptionist that I wanted to adopt an adult Himalayan cat. She said, "Oh, you're in luck! One of our clients just got a dog, and she has to give away her cat because the two don't get along. She hates to lose her cat, but her daughter is completely attached to the dog. She just this afternoon placed a 'Free Cat' notice on our bulletin board! It's a female Himalayan named Precious, and she's had all her shots and everything."

That Saturday, I met with Precious's owner, and she was so happy that her darling cat had found an appreciative new owner.

And I was happy that my mental image of my perfect home—complete with a cat curled up in front of the fireplace—had come true.

Equal Opportunity Laws

At this point, you may be thinking, "Okay, so this author has had some amazing coincidences occur," or "Well, the author knows how to manifest. But that would never happen to ME!" The spiritual principles and laws that allow me to instantly manifest apply equally to every single person—no exceptions!

Just as everybody who lifts weights will eventually develop muscle tone, everybody who uses principles of manifestation *will* realize their dreams. Spiritual laws never discriminate against anyone, never bar anyone from usage. It's like electrical power—no matter who you are, if you flip on a light switch, the lights always go on. Electricity doesn't care who turns it on; it merely obeys commands. Spiritual principles are no different.

Spiritual laws of manifestation are also like laws of mathematics. Two plus two always equals four, without exception. It doesn't matter what the age, sex, appearance, race, history, or ethnicity of the person is who adds two plus two. The result is always the same, because mathematical law—like spiritual law—is divinely and perfectly ordered. Trust that it will work for you, because trust is a necessary component of making it work.

"WE FOLLOWED OUR INTUITION HOME"

With two teenage children and two foster children living with them, Terry and Betty Fennel felt cramped in their small three-bedroom home. The thought of moving seemed financially unfeasible, but Terry's spiritual beliefs helped the family manifest their dreams into reality.

Terry described the details of his dream house to a Realtor: A pool for the teenagers to enjoy in the summer, a satellite dish, a spa, at least five bedrooms, in the country but close to a school bus, a garage, space for a home office, room to play basketball, and a master bedroom with a sitting area.

The Realtor listened and exclaimed, "Terry, I *have* your house!" He was correct; the home had all the features Terry had described, along with four acres and a fish pond. But the price was astronomical—their monthly house payments would quadruple! Terry and Betty would need a miracle to afford the new home. Well, they got one.

The couple loved the home and made an offer, which the seller immediately accepted. But instead of being elated over their purchase, Terry and Betty felt confused. On the one hand, they both *knew* that this was the house they would live in. However, a strong gut feeling warned them against buying the house for so much money.

One thing after another went wrong. Foster-child program officials wouldn't approve the home right away. The fire marshal demanded a complete remodeling of the home. Even the county zoning commission said that the home's zoning wouldn't allow foster children. Terry and Betty recognized the roadblocks as confirmation that they should follow their instincts and cancel the deal. Reluctantly, they signed paperwork to abolish the purchase agreement.

Later, as the couple discussed the "house that got away," Betty again affirmed that she knew that somehow they would live in that home. She told Terry, "Everyone will win if we get it! We'll have a beautiful place to live, the agent will get a handsome commission, the sellers will get their money, our children will have enough room, and even the foster-child program will benefit by our having a better home for more foster kids. On the other hand, if we don't get the home, then everyone will lose."

Terry reminded Betty that they had just canceled the deal, but she persisted in affirming that somehow they'd own the house. "We will get the house because God will be our co-signer," said Betty.

Two weeks later, the Realtor called excitedly to say that he'd worked out arrangements so that the couple could now afford to buy their house for the exact amount Terry had earlier mentioned.

The couple's earlier gut feeling suddenly made sense. They had been guided to buy the house, but not at its original asking price. Terry, Betty, and all of their children happily purchased their dream home for the exact price they had envisioned when they'd originally delineated the details of their ideal home!

Having It All

A client of mine named Suzanne was skeptical when I explained these manifesting principles to her. "That's the kind of thing my husband always talks about," she said. It was a phrase I'd hear a lot from Suzanne throughout our therapy sessions. She didn't believe one word of any discussion about the power of thoughts, visualizations, affirmations, and the like. *Hokey garbage* was the term I believe she used.

That all changed the day her husband, Roy, brought home what, to Suzanne, was the equivalent of magic beans that turned into a giant beanstalk. Here's how Suzanne described the experience to me:

"Roy and I have always dreamed of building a house on a bluff overlooking the Pacific Ocean. We've lived in a dark canyon a couple miles from the ocean for years. Even though I wanted this as much as Roy, I never believed it would actually come true. I mean, we're not exactly rich! But Roy never doubted that we'd get our dream house.

"He'd always tell me how he was using affirmations and visualization to picture us owning land on a flat lot overlooking the sea. I'd just roll my eyes and think, Dream on! But today, Roy did it! I mean, I'm just floored!"

At a land auction that day, Roy had successfully bid on a choice chunk of flat land overlooking the ocean. It was exactly as he'd envisioned, purchased for the exact cost he'd affirmed. Suzanne's skepticism about manifesting vanished, which was what Roy had also affirmed!

I could fill a book with examples of manifestations experienced by my friends, family, clients, and myself! I know, without a doubt, that these principles work when they are properly applied. Here are some other brief examples:

✦ A friend of mine named Dan wanted a hang glider. He hung a photo in his office of his favorite type of glider, and stared at it each day. Within a month of hanging the photo, Dan's neighbor mentioned that he was giving up the hang-gliding sport. And, oh, by the way, would Dan be interested in having his hang glider? The neighbor insisted on giving it to Dan, and it was the exact model and color of the hang glider in Dan's office picture!

✦ A woman I know named Debra was tired of the singles market. A single parent, she wanted to be married to a great man who'd love her kids. She wrote a "dream man list" with all her desired characteristics, and she carried it in her wallet. Every day, Debra looked at the list, knowing without a doubt that she would manifest this person. She did! Within one month, she began dating Chris—an extremely handsome and successful man who matched every characteristic on her list to a tee. Today, they are in love and happily married.

✦ This is a "smaller" manifestation, but impressive, nonetheless. Several Christmases before I'd met him, my husband Michael was doing some very last-minute gift wrapping. Everything was going fine until he ran out of tape! Since it was Christmas Day, the only store open where he could buy tape was several miles away. Michael, who is a strong believer in manifestation, declared to the universe that he *must* have tape. His intuition then prompted him to walk outside the house. There—lying in the middle of the street—was a huge roll of transparent tape. Michael still has the roll of what he calls his "miracle tape."

In No Time at All!

The point of all these illustrations is to show that "rules" about time and achieving dreams are subject to artistic license. We are free to rewrite rules concerning time to suit our needs. Ironically, by relaxing about time pressures, we reduce energy-draining anger, tension, and guilt. Thus, we're more energized and able to accomplish more.

Bottom line: Refuse to accept negative ideas about what you can't accomplish or what's impossible. Don't even talk to negative people while your dreams are still in the fragile incubation stage!

My clinical practice shows that anyone—no matter what their background, age, appearance, sex, income, education, or religion— can succeed in getting their heart's desire. Will you give it a sincere effort and see for yourself?

It's Okay to Come Out and Play

Many people got caught up in the materialistic frenzy of the 1980s. Some loaded up on real estate or stock market investments and then lost everything when the market turned sour. I've talked to many people who experienced financial, emotional, and morale crashes during the late 1980s and early 1990s. They invested so much in real estate holdings—their life savings and credit, their dreams for a bright retirement, their hopes about their personal strength and livelihood, and their trust in themselves to decide. When they lost their financial footing through real estate depreciation, economic inflation, and company mergers and layoffs, they lost something even more valuable—their faith.

This disheartening turn of events is partially responsible for the current emerging spiritual renaissance. We've learned to distrust material investments and are turning to something that is trustworthy and lasting: spirit. The trouble is, while we're searching for and studying our spiritual paths, we still have bills to pay. Many of us have children to raise and other pressing responsibilities.

Still, during those moments when we glimpse the bliss of spirituality—during yoga, meditation, seminars, reading, or walking— we sigh, "There must be a way that I can extend my spiritual serenity while fulfilling my adulthood responsibilities." Many have fantasies of running off to India, Tibet, or Peru to study with spiritual masters.

For the past several years, I've received a steady stream of questions from my clients, people who read my books, and talk-show audience members, about how to make serious money in meaningful ways. Here are some of the questions I hear most often:

+ "I'd love to have a creative job (author, artist, actress, etc.), but I don't know how to go about getting started. How can I know if I have enough talent to make money doing what I love?"

+ "I've always wanted to be a healer, but I feel I'm too old to go to medical school or get a Ph.D. What other ways can I work in a healing field?"

✦ "I feel so trapped! I can't stand the job I've got, but I don't know how else I can make enough money to pay all my bills. What can I do?"

✦ "I'm not clear about what my divine path is. I really try to listen in meditation, but I can't hear a thing! What's the problem?"

✦ "Every time I even think about changing careers, I get really scared. I don't want to make a mistake; how can I be really sure what the right thing is for me to do?"

All these questions are perfectly normal. We may not "want it all," but we do want more than we presently have. While we've outgrown the '80s fixations with BMW's and food processors, we still dream of financial independence and free time to spend with our families and with ourselves. We're not asking for the lifestyle of the rich and famous, just some financial and emotional security.

"I'm so sick of working all the time, when I have nothing to show for it!" says 42-year-old Emilee, an office manager and mother of two. The daily grind of getting the children to day care, commuting to work, and enduring stomach-churning company politics is eroding Emilee's confidence and energy.

Some people in Emilee's position simply give up hope of ever having a better life. They numb their ambitions with sarcasm and apathy, saying, "What's the use of even trying?"

Others—like you, perhaps—take a different, more productive approach. You probably already know, deep down, that you can create a better world for yourself—a secure life with higher income, meaningful work, and fulfilling relationships. That's why you investigate and research ways to improve your day-to-day existence.

Think-and-Grow-Rich Theories

In reviewing and reading the many books on prosperity that are on the market today, you can see a common thread running through each: "Hold positive thoughts about what you want, believe that you will receive it, and you will have it." This sentiment comes straight from the Bible, and is echoed in almost every major religion.

Scriptures invariably stress the importance of living in a state of gratitude. Ask to have your material needs and comforts met, but be grateful for what you currently have, and know that God answers every need. Let's say you currently live in a small, sparsely furnished apartment and drive an unreliable car. You would like to live in a more comfortable home and own a safer automobile. Being miserable about your current state would block you from receiving greater good. However, asking for your desired changes and lovingly knowing that they are on their way ensures their physical manifestation.

Many motivational and success books underemphasize an important point that the Bible and other spiritual works emphatically spell out: You can't just sit in your apartment and dream about money and expect a bushel of dollars to drop through your chimney and into your living room. You must first help yourself and do some useful work. Your gut feelings will guide you as to what work to perform each day.

Yet, some motivational books imply that all you need to do is think and visualize and *voilà*! No wonder people get turned off to motivational books and tapes. The spiritual process of success involves meditating for rich ideas that translate into action, which then results in abundance. One reason you may have been suspicious or wary about "think-and-grow-rich sentiments" is because you knew, deep down, that success requires some effort.

Without a cause, there can be no effect. Money is the effect, and God, your positive thoughts, and work are the combined cause. This all fits perfectly together:

1.   As you focus on thoughts of accomplishment and abundance, your mind automatically relaxes and lets go of fear. This causes a shift in your frequency that frees your creative-thinking capacity. It also releases your inner guide and angels (whom your fear blocks) so they can intervene and help you through miraculous "coincidences."

2.   Because your mind and emotions are unencumbered by worries, you generate many ideas and, as a result, you are more apt to act upon these ideas and believe in yourself.

3.   These action steps, taken collectively, are the causes that create the effect of manifesting your goals.

The Desire Triangle

What you want in your life is irrelevant, because the process of attaining any goal is identical for all goals. Attaining health is identical to the process of attaining wealth, which is identical to the process of attracting love. Although there is no difference in manifesting various goals, many people's lives are unevenly distributed. For example, one person may have a fat bank account but a loveless marriage. Another person may be enjoying a rich romantic life but has a miserable job. Still another may be happily married with a great career but finds her health or weight is a continual struggle.

I think of the three life areas most often involved in goal-setting—love, wealth, and health—as a triangle. It seems that very few people feel successful in all three tips of the triangle. Usually, most people have one or two areas in which they excel, and the third area is dangling in the wind.

Could this be a fear of being too perfect, of alienating others if we don't have some human foible or flaw? In talking with some very successful and powerful people, I have found that this is often the case—especially with women. Oprah Winfrey shared with me her belief that women may fear becoming *too* strong or successful, because strong women intimidate some people. I agree with her.

I'm not suggesting that we try to have it all, or become a superwoman or superman. That type of lifestyle leads to burnout, frustration, and dissatisfaction with life. After all, joy comes from fulfilling our divine purpose, not from accumulating possessions or accomplishments. However, I am recommending a steady flow toward goals in the three important areas of health, work, and love.

All three areas interact with one another closely. Our satisfaction at work and home affects our health. Our health affects our work and home lives. Our income may rise and fall depending on our level of health, and whether we're depressed or emotionally stable. Our moods influence all of the relationships in our lives, and so on.

The triangle intertwines and is interdependent. Yet, many people find that maintaining success in more than one or two areas is difficult, even impossible. However, it doesn't have to be this way. On close examination, we always find an underlying decision that creates dissatisfaction in one life area. Common occurrences are:

+ Believing it's not right, moral, or spiritually correct to want money.
+ A habit of settling for whatever circumstances drift into your life.
+ Viewing a happy love life as an unrealistic or superficial goal.
+ Seeing radiant health as unattainable because of beliefs such as "I'm too old," "I have kids," "I don't have enough time or money," and so on.

Although we may hold firm beliefs to the contrary, one tip of this Love-Career-Health triangle is no more difficult to attain or maintain than any of the other tips. However, our beliefs do influence our experiences, and any of the above-listed beliefs could block you. If you've achieved progress or success in one tip of the triangle, please know that you can experience the same results in other life areas as well.

The Journey, Not the Finish Line

In reality, we never complete, attain, or finish the goals of the soul. That implies stopping at the end of something. The goal *is* the goal—it's a way of organizing time and behavior so we can continually create. We are, after all, eternal creators.

Being *in* the goal, not following behind it, is your soul's goal. Whether your goal is to be a great artist, novelist, or actor, the goal is a vehicle for helping others to fulfill their soul's goal. But perhaps you're not really sure what you want. Maybe you keep changing your mind from day to day. Or you're afraid of making the "wrong" choice, and then being trapped or disappointed.

It's vital to know what you want and to clearly understand your Divine Purpose. In the next chapter, we'll stop and catch our breath long enough to listen to that still, small voice within that whispers to us about our dreams. Then we'll write them down!

POINTS TO REMEMBER

🔊 It's not enough to merely *think* about growing rich or achieving other goals; action must follow thought. God helps those who help themselves.

🔊 Our thoughts about time create our experiences. It's important to replace limited thinking concerning time with expanded and positive thoughts that affirm that there is an abundance of time.

🔊 Love relationships, careers, and health are all similarly accomplished goals, like three equal tips of a triangle. If you have achieved success in one of these areas, you can accomplish your goals in the other areas.

🔊 The soul needs continual growth, and so the goals of the soul are never completed or finished.

IDENTIFYING YOUR DIVINE PURPOSE

"One always has time enough, if one will apply it well."
— JOHANN WOLFGANG VON GOETHE,
GERMAN AUTHOR, 1749–1832

Teresa, a 37-year-old office manager, sat in my psychotherapy office complaining of a vague sense of unhappiness. "There's something missing from my life," she sighed, struggling to put her emptiness into words.

My words stumped Teresa when I asked, "What do you want?"

She knew she was unhappy and unfulfilled. Teresa didn't like her job, the car she drove, or the quality of her marriage, yet she had no idea what alternatives would please her. So our first two sessions concentrated on Teresa deciding exactly what she wanted. This helped her see the many choices available to her, and opened the way for her to make positive changes.

It's not enough to know what you *don't* want. That's like going into a restaurant and telling the waiter, "I don't want steak, hamburgers, or fish," and hoping he'll bring you a meal you'll like. The only way to get what you want is by *knowing* what you want and then specifically ordering it.

"I don't *know* what I want!" I hear this statement a lot, and understand that it's difficult, even frightening, to pinpoint goals and aspirations. Committing to one choice requires eliminating other options. That's why I'm devoting this chapter to the science of goal-setting and helping you specifically design a mental picture of what you really want.

Goals Are a Necessity, Not a Luxury

Unless you have your own clear idea of how you want your life to look, you won't feel in charge of your time. "Those who don't have goals are forever doomed to work for those who do," author Brian Tracy once told me. Spend a moment with the last sentence. When you don't have goals, you give your free time to people who are all-too-anxious to control your energies. Instead of spending your time in fulfilling ways, your days are monopolized with accomplishing someone else's dreams.

Almost all successful people start in a similar fashion—with clear definitions of their values and goals. Every one of us knows, deep down, what's important to us and what we want. It's just that sometimes those dreams get buried, thwarted, or forgotten. Sometimes we don't realize that it's possible to work less and have more. Let's dig all your dreams out, dust them off, and polish them, because the time to work on them is NOW!

Many people find it frightening to examine their dreams closely. It's tempting to say, "I'll set goals tomorrow, when I feel more energetic and have more time." Most people procrastinate goal-setting forever, and then can't understand why their lives and their bank accounts seem unfulfilling and empty.

Usually, we delay setting goals due to the fear of losing something or somebody:

+ Jacqueline feared that her husband would leave her if she followed her dream and spent three nights a week at law school.

+ Marie was afraid that her children would suffer if she spent time taking yoga and meditation classes.

+ Robert worried that if he got the house he always dreamed of, he might someday go broke and *lose* the house—and that would be painful and humiliating.

+ Cassandra wanted to spend more time with her baby daughter, but her real estate brokerage kept her on call for client showings around the clock. She wondered how she could spend more time with her baby without quitting her job and going on public assistance.

+ Although Julie's schedule was overbooked, she spent an hour each night on the telephone listening to her friend Pam complain about her love life and finances. Julie would have loved to skip the nightly phone calls, but she feared that Pam would be angry and hurt.

+ James procrastinated sending his manuscript to publishers because he dreaded rejection.

+ Anna hesitated asking for a raise, presuming that her boss would say no, or even fire her. She also believed, deep down, that she didn't deserve more money.

+ Kathy agonized over flunking out of college, so she procrastinated applying for admission. After all, Kathy's mother had always told her, "Women don't need to go to college; they just need a husband."

+ Brenda feared leaving her emotionally abusive, alcoholic husband, Mark. She was afraid of being alone and enduring financial struggles, and worried that she'd never find another mate.

✦ Kevin was afraid of choosing the "wrong" career, so he delayed deciding and instead stayed in his unfulfilling, low-paying job. Kevin told himself, "Someday, I'll know what I want to do for a living. But not yet."

✦ Stella wouldn't ever take time away from her family to go to the gym and work on her physical health. "That would be selfish," she told herself.

Doubts, fears, and insecurities paralyzed these women and men. They knew they wanted better lives, but they were afraid that the price they'd have to pay was too high.

"One-dimensional goal-setting" is the false belief that to attain one dream, you have to give up something else. Healthy goal-setting transcends focusing on just one aspect of your life. It means deciding what you want your *entire* life to look and feel like. To me, "having it all" means having plenty of free time, rather than plenty of possessions. So, choose the best love life, career life, spiritual life, family life, and personal life you can!

The first fear to let go of during goal-setting is the one that says, "Will my loved ones leave me or be angry with me if I focus on myself for a while?" The answer is that when you win, everybody wins. It's an aphorism based in total truth: you can only give love when you first feel love for yourself and your life. It's not only *okay* to take care of your own needs—it is essential!

Unfulfilled people eventually become resentful of everyone around them. The toxic vapor of resentment permeates every crevice of life, hardening stern wrinkles into facial features and twisting the stomach with knots and acid. Let's replace any resentment with satisfaction, and rejuvenate the emotional, spiritual, and physical health in your life and your family's life.

Healthy Goal-Setting and Goal-Getting

"There is no greater demonstration of the power of faith than to decide what you're going to do, and to become determined in your own mind that you're going to do it."
— NAPOLEON HILL, AUTHOR OF
THINK AND GROW RICH

Anyone can achieve goals; we all accomplish them every day. However, many people set their goals too low and settle for too little. There's no better time than right now to clarify and set your goals. Even if you have set goals in the past, you've got to update your aspirations continually. If you haven't written down your goals within the past five days, take a moment right now to get a pen and some paper. If you've never before set down your goals on paper, you will love how rapidly this seemingly simple act creates successes. For the moment, please suspend any concerns about "how" you will accomplish these goals—that comes later.

◆ ◆ ◆

I'm using the word *goal* interchangeably with the words *desire, dream, aspiration, function, purpose,* and *mission.* I realize that the word *goal* is out of vogue, and even has negative connotations left over from the fast-track '80s when many people maxed out their credit limits to purchase fancy cars, houses, and appliances.

By goals, I mean "what you want to have, be, or do." One of your goals will probably be to simplify your life. A wonderful goal is to take charge of your free time, so you can really relax, meditate, enjoy your family, and feel rested.

This is a very different approach to goal-setting, as my client Wanda discovered. Wanda told me that during the '80s she had spent thousands of dollars on audiocassettes and books about goal-setting. Since she hadn't fulfilled her desires, she'd thrown away all the tapes and books! When Wanda began working with me, she balked when I asked her to write down her desires. "I tried that before, and it didn't work!" she protested.

Still, I urged her to complete this step. Afterward, Wanda admitted that her new list of goals was completely different from those she had in the past. Wanda's previous goals were what she thought she "should" want. This time, though, her goals were from her heart and soul. Here is her story:

Wanda was a sweet and caring person with an artistic flair, yet during the 1970s and '80s, she had chosen goals completely out of line with her personality and interests. For example, she'd worked for five years as a police officer, patrolling the tough streets of Los Angeles by foot.

When Wanda realized that police work didn't suit her, she switched to pursuing an M.B.A. degree. However, the studies bored her to tears, so she quit and became an insurance sales agent. Again, Wanda was frustrated because she didn't like to network and cold-call. She was bereft of hope and disgusted, and it was obvious that none of her "motivational" tapes or books had helped at all!

When I asked Wanda to describe the kind of life she *really* wanted, she blinked at me with disbelief. She kept asking, "Are you sure it's okay if I write down everything I want? Are you sure I won't be setting myself up for disappointment?" When I reassured her that she could manifest her heart's true desires, Wanda got honest with herself.

She told me how, for the past ten years, she'd taken biannual vacations to Peru, from where her family originated. "It's amazing, but the moment I get off the plane in Peru, I feel like a completely different person. Here, I must use a cane to walk because of pain in my knees. Yet in Peru, I can walk pain free without the cane! Here, I can't control my appetite and I can't stand to exercise. Over in Peru, though, I love to take long walks along the trails, and I eat only fresh fruits and vegetables. Here, I keep to myself. But in Peru, I've got some great friends and a wonderful boyfriend. I dream about opening an employment agency in Peru. I've even picked out a building site, and I have enough money saved to sustain me for a year, but I don't know…"

Wanda's voice trailed off, as she looked down. Our following sessions focused on the fears that blocked Wanda from admitting and fulfilling her dream of moving to Peru and opening an employment agency. Wanda's first block—a deep confusion about whether she "deserved" to have this dream—was a product of her parents continually telling her, "You're a loser."

Wanda's second fear was that if she accomplished these dreams, they might eventually slip away. What if her boyfriend rejected her after she moved there? What if she couldn't find a suitable place to live? She had a million "what ifs" that prevented her from admitting how deeply she desired this goal.

When she forced herself to sit and write down what she really wanted, though, the logic of it all surprised Wanda! After all, she had no ties to keep her in Los Angeles, and she'd saved enough money to make the move, open her agency, and survive the initial slow months of business. Her health, friendships, love life, and passions all pointed in the same direction: Peru.

This time, because she'd set goals based on her heart and soul, Wanda's goal-setting resulted in true emotional, physical, spiritual, and financial fulfillment!

You Will Be Guided

Like Wanda, your soul already knows what your *true* desires are. Your true desires are those that will give you the joy and freedom

you seek. This is different from seeking joy through the accumu-
lation of material wealth. True desires are based on giving to the
world, while ego-based desires are only concerned with getting.
Ironically, you end up getting more from true desires than from
ego-based desires. The sooner you surrender your ego-based desires, the sooner you'll enjoy yourself.

Consider your deepest, most secret desires for one moment. Ask
yourself, "Where did this desire come from?" If the thought of
fulfilling that desire brings you joy, then this is a clue that it is a
true desire and your divine assignment. A divine assignment is the
role you agreed to fulfill during your lifetime. It's a role that makes
the world a better place. You will experience the most incredible
happiness and comfort by accepting this divine assignment. However, you might hesitate, feeling unqualified to accept it. Please
know this, though: *you are supremely qualified to fulfill your Divine
Purpose.*

The instant you surrender to your true desires and your intuition's
urges, your life will never be the same. Miraculous coincidences,
such as phone calls, "chance meetings," books falling off of book-
shelves, and intuitive urges will appear out of the ethers! You will
also receive specific instructions on how to fulfill your divine assignment, and you will receive all the time, support, money, and
help that you need.

Your instructions will be given to you one or two steps at a time,
so don't worry that you won't know how to handle your assignment
in the future. When you follow and complete your intuition's first
instruction, your next set of instructions will be given to you, and
so on. In a short time, you'll learn to trust these intuitive messages
and will joyfully look forward to receiving and following each one.

As a person who has tried to find joy through material routes, I
know that lasting happiness and security only come from staying
on the spiritual path that my intuition carves out for me. Fancy
homes and material possessions are fine, but they don't provide a
fraction of the joy compared to being in love with my life and ful-

filling my divine assignment. Love is my most prized possession, one that multiplies as I give it away. And giving love, after all, is my divine assignment. It's yours, as well, in whatever form your intuition guides you!

POINTS TO REMEMBER

⋧ Unclear goals create unclear results. You need to know where you're going, and have faith that you will get there. Your intuition has been nagging at you to get moving on your goals. It's time to listen and obey your intuition, because that's how you'll get the joy, freedom, and security you want and deserve.

⋧ Everyone has goals, because everyone has a divine assignment. You'll clearly understand your divine assignment by listening to and obeying your intuition.

⋧ You are *very, very* qualified to fulfill your divine assignment. These assignments are never given by mistake or accident.

⋧ Every time you finish one step of your intuitive instructions, you will be given another set of them. Don't fret about not knowing what to do in the future; you will be guided every day of your life.

⋧   ⋧   ⋧

UNLEASHING YOUR DREAMS

"The ultimate of being successful is the luxury of giving yourself the time to do what you want to do."
— MARY LEONTYNE PRICE (1927–),
AMERICAN OPERA STAR

Take a moment to ask yourself, "What do I want to be, have, and do?" Suspend any doubts and fears about being unrealistic, and pretend that a philanthropist will finance any ambition you have. Write down detailed descriptions about your ideal life—everything from your dream house, to your ideal relationship, to relaxation and play time, to your perfect career choice.

Let your mind relax and wander as you crystallize vivid images of your dream life. Think about other people's lifestyles that you've admired, and write down which parts you'd like to have and live yourself.

Unclear goals create unclear and therefore, unsatisfying, outcomes. The old aphorism is so true: "You can't hit a target that you can't see." Until your desires are specific and completely clear, you won't be happy with the results they bring. You've got to fill in all the blanks in your description of a dream life—or risk having others fill in those blanks for you. Leave nothing to chance, and decide on everything you want.

Imagine that your philanthropic billionaire tells you, "If you write a clear description of what you want, I will pay for everything." All that your underwriter asks of you is a specific description of your dream life.

Let yourself go, and come up with goals that really excite you! *Since you can't not create,* you may as well come up with goals that create a happier you. If you've tried this method unsuccessfully in the past, please don't doubt the process. Perhaps it didn't work for you because you wrote goals you really didn't believe you'd attain, or that you didn't really want to have in the first place. As we discussed in the last chapter, your soul already knows what you want because it knows what you need in order to fulfill your divine assignment. For example, if your divine assignment is to be a healer, your soul knows what you need in the way of education, material goods, and experiences. Those are the items to clarify and write on your list.

> *Your Divine Purpose—and all of the things, people, money, shelter, and support you need in order to fulfill your assignment—is your goal.*

If you feel stuck or unsure about what you want, that's okay. You may first need to follow the steps in Part Five of this book, so that your inner guide can give you a clearer picture of what type of life would most fulfill you.

As you read on and practice the steps in this book, you'll probably find that you want to change or add to your list. That's okay, too! This list is a great jumping-off place, one that I highly recommend. The act of writing down what you want is one of the most important steps in fulfilling your heart's desire. In fact, it is so powerful that it is practically an indispensable step.

Goals for Life

I've written down my desires and goals for many years, always with amazing results.

I once believed that goal-setting was just a tool for career and financial success. Goal-setting helped me become published at age 30, a bestselling author appearing on national television at age 31, and the owner of a great house, car, and furnishings. Nevertheless, while I was enjoying career and financial success, other areas of my life were suffering.

Half out of desperation and half out of curiosity, I decided to apply goal-setting to my love, family, health, and spiritual lives. I was shocked, but it worked! For example, I wanted to be in a relationship. Unfortunately, the men I was meeting and dating had very different values and lifestyles than I was looking for in a life partner.

So, I halfheartedly tried to spiritually manifest a love relationship. As I wrote earlier, lukewarm visualizations create lukewarm results. And, oh boy, did I get a lukewarm result with the man that I manifested! My halfhearted attempt consisted of deciding, "I want to meet a romantic man who will give me red roses." I didn't include any other details about what I wanted. Big mistake! It's like ordering a sandwich and telling the waiter to put whatever he wants between the two slices of bread. When ordering anything—especially the important stuff, such as a love partner—we need to be *very* specific.

Anyway, about two days after I'd affirmed my desire for a rose-bearing boyfriend, I met John the accountant. He was pleasant looking, nice to be around, and successful. And John was definitely into giving roses! Apparently, I went overboard on my manifestations by emphasizing roses, because a week after we started dating, John was inundating my office with florist deliveries. My desk, bookshelf, and filing cabinet were overflowing with gorgeous vases of red, red roses. It got to the point where my secretary was making fun of the daily floral deliveries. I felt like Mickey Mouse in the movie *Fantasia*, with an endless procession of roses coming toward me.

John's romantic gestures would have been welcomed were it not for my neglecting to manifest one important feature in the relationship: chemistry. Unfortunately, I felt absolutely none with John. Zero, zip, nada. My head told me that he was a great guy, but my heart couldn't even bring me to hold his hand or kiss him.

I vowed that my next manifestation would have all the essential details So, I went out on a limb and wrote down every quality and characteristic that I wanted in a man and a relationship. Many of the men I'd dated had different views of marriage than my own—they either wanted to get married immediately, or they did not want to get married at all. Well, I wanted to be married, but I also wanted a long engagement. So one of the items on my list was, "I want to get engaged right away, and be engaged for two years before getting married." My detailed list was two pages long!

Then I used the other components of goal-setting that had worked so well in my career: visualization and faith. I'd close my eyes and *know* that the man of my dreams was looking for me as fervently as I was looking for him. For some reason, every time I'd close my eyes and think of him, I would see a white kitchen countertop.

A couple of days after I made the list, I received strong gut feelings to go to certain places and call certain people out of my ordinary routine. These events led up to my walking into a small French restaurant near my home, a place where I normally would never go since I avoid the high-fat sauces that are particular to French cuisine.

As I entered the restaurant, a tall man nearly bumped into me. We exchanged "Hellos" and began talking. Within an hour, I knew that this man was the person I'd described on my goal-setting sheet. Michael and I have been together, happily in love, ever since. And just as I visualized, we were engaged for two years and got married on the third anniversary of our meeting. We even ate our wedding dinner at the French restaurant where we first met. The fascinating part about all this is that Michael also had a goal-setting list about his dream mate, and I was that person!

Whenever I feel stagnant or depressed, it's usually because I'm not writing, reviewing, and updating my goals. One thing I want to emphasize to you is that *there are no limits to the joy and success you and your family can experience*, except those limits you place upon yourself.

In a blank writing journal, detail your heart's desires. Do not let any fears or self-judgments of being "materialistic," "unrealistic," or "superficial" block you from putting honest answers on each page. Remember that many of your desires originated on a spiritual plane, and there is nothing to be embarrassed about in desiring a more comfortable life.

On the other hand, write down only those dreams you honestly want. In other words, don't write that you want a five-story mansion just because you think you "should" want a big house. If, in reality, you'd prefer a cozy condominium, then say so.

Write down the details that are important to you. As you'll read in Part Five, it's best to hold a concrete image of these desired goals during your meditation periods, and to feel grateful and confident that spiritual law is now delivering these desires to you.

Here are some questions to ask yourself as you describe and define each important area of your life:

— *My free time and personal life:* What activities would I like to be doing more often? How would I like to spend my free time? Do I want to take more vacations (to where, how often, and what type)? Do I want more time to meditate, relax, or sleep? How much time? Who would be with me during my free time? Where would I be? Do I want a simpler life? A more stable life? What is important to me?

— *My career:* What career would I switch to if I won the lottery today? If I found out that I only had three months to live? What dream career do I someday hope to have? What activities do I see myself doing in my career? Is there a class I can take or a book I can read today? Do I need new equipment or a facility for my new career? How would I feel about taking one small step toward the fulfillment of this career? What is that small step, so I can write it down on my goal sheet? Are there parts of my present career that I can change right now, to loosen my schedule? If I am climbing the company ladder, am I really sure this is what I want? What is my primary reason for working? What is my secondary reason for working? Is my time organized toward the fulfillment of these goals?

— *My love life*: What type of relationship do I want? Is it more like a friendship or like a passionate affair? Which qualities and characteristics are important to me in a partner: employed, self-employed, a student, an independent type, a hard worker, artistic, businesslike, fancy, casual, appreciative, educated, relaxed, confident, friendly, outgoing, humorous, sensuous, thoughtful, honest, monogamous, romantic, studious, supportive, loving, spiritual, religious, family oriented, childless, athletic, vegetarian, casual drinker, nonsmoker, sober, sociable, quiet, demure, petite, strong, tall, well-built, humble, serious, homespun, domestic, gourmet, confident, talkative, cuddly, morning person, night person?

— *My income, expenses, and finances*: How much debt do I want to carry, and for what purpose? Would I like to pay off one or more of my credit accounts? By when? How much money do I want to make next month? Next year? Five years from now? What expenses do I want to cut down or cut out?

— *My home and community:* What changes do I want to make in my current living environment? Do I want to fix up my home or yard? Do I want to move? What is my ideal home like? Where is it? What is my personal corner or room like? Does it have a garden, pool, or pond? Is it near the ocean, a lake, the desert, or mountains? Is it in the city or the country? What part of the world do I live in? What is my neighborhood like? What community projects am I involved in, if any?

— *My spiritual life*: How much time do I want to devote to spiritual practices, such as meditation, classes, church, volunteer work, and so on? What books do I want to read? What classes do I want to take? What spiritual teachers, authors, or leaders do I want to meet, listen to, and/or work with? What spiritual power places do I want to visit, with whom, and when? What spiritual projects do I want to work on? What spiritual gift do I want to give to others?

— *My health and fitness:* What changes do I want to make in my health and fitness? How much time per day or week do I want to spend exercising? What type of exercise program would I most enjoy and benefit from? Where would I exercise? With whom? What physical healings do I want? If I were to manifest my true natural state of perfect health right now, what would my body be like? About what weight or fat percentage would my body feel comfortable and healthy being? What types of foods would be in my regular diet? What would my ideal sleeping pattern be? How would I deal with stress or tension? What unnecessary stressors do I want to get rid of? What toxins (emotional or physical) can I eliminate from my diet or life?

— *My family life*: What type of family life do I want? What about children? How much time do I want to spend with my kids? What do I want to teach or share with them? How can I be closer to my family and/or spend more quality time with them? What type of relationship do I want with my parents? With my siblings? With my in-laws? With my other relatives? Do I need to forgive any family member? How do I want to relate to my spouse or ex-spouse with respect to the upbringing of our children? What type of family life feels right to me?

— *My friends and social life*: How much time do I want to spend with my friends and acquaintances? What types of friendships do I want to encourage? Do I prefer one or two close friends, or a group of friends? What qualities and characteristics do my friends and I have? What activities would I most enjoy undertaking with them? What changes do I want to make with the people I currently socialize with? Do I need to set or maintain boundaries with any people currently in my life? Do I need to forgive any of my present or past friends? How much time do I want to spend on the telephone with my friends? What are my true beliefs about giving help to my friends?

— *My hobbies and recreational life*: What do I most like to do? What did I like to do for fun when I was a kid? When I was a teenager? What new hobbies or sports do I want to learn? How do I want to spend my weekends and other free time? What equipment, trips, classes, or memberships do I want to purchase? When will I use them? Where? How often? With whom?

— *My education:* What do I want to learn? What topics fascinate me? Do I want to earn a degree or certificate? What would be fun, interesting, profitable, healthy, and/or beneficial for me to learn? What institutions or teachers do I want to learn from? What steps can I take today to propel me toward these goals?

— *My possessions:* What types of possessions do I want or
need in order to fulfill my divine function? What objects
would make my life easier, safer, or more enjoyable? What
types of furniture, clothing, cars, recreational vehicles, jew-
elry, equipment, toys, or other possessions have I always
wanted? What possessions are weighing me down? What
would I like to get rid of? Do I have anything I'd like to sell,
donate, barter, or trade?

When you've answered these questions for yourself, you'll be
well on the way to setting healthy goals that will enrich and enhance your life!

POINTS TO REMEMBER

ᏅᎯ Healthy goal-setting involves all aspects of your life, including leisure time, family time, love life, health/fitness/weight,
spirituality, and career/finances.

ᏅᎯ Goal-setting is a way to honestly admit to acknowledge
all those things and conditions that you've always wanted.
The most important process in healthy goal-setting is self-
honesty.

ᏅᎯ   ᏅᎯ   ᏅᎯ

Overcoming Fears and Other Blocks to Success

HOW FEAR CREATES PROCRASTINATION

"The best way to prepare for tomorrow is to make today's consciousness serene and harmonious. All other good things will follow upon that."

— EMMET FOX (1886–1951), AUTHOR OF
THE SERMON ON THE MOUNT

I live next-door to a golden retriever named Katie. Whenever I'm on my patio, Katie comes over to play. Anyone who knows golden retrievers already knows this breed's favorite pastime: chasing and retrieving balls.

Katie always greets me with a green tennis ball in her jaws, and her eyes plead for me to toss her the ball. I clap my hands and say, "Drop the ball, Katie!" so I can throw it for her.

"Grrrrr." Katie playfully shakes her head as if to say, "You want this ball, but you can't have it, nyah, nyah!"

"But Katie, how can I throw you the ball if you won't let go?" Although her greatest pleasure comes from chasing balls, Katie doesn't like to let go of the ball. Her behavior reminds me of my clients who know which goals they want, but who hesitate to drop whatever stands in their way. They crave happiness, but they won't surrender the fear or habits that block them.

How sad when a dream is within reach, yet we clutch tightly to obstacles that hinder our accomplishments. Let's not do that to ourselves any longer! For us, the consequences of refusing to drop our obstacles are more serious than they are for Katie. The balls we clutch so tightly can lock us into unfulfilling jobs, tight budgets, miserable relationships, and—worst of all—unserved purposes. So, let's identify the balls we carry, and then drop them!

> *"How true this is: no one can give unto us but our-selves, and no one can rob us but ourselves."*
>
> — ERNEST HOLMES (1887–1960), AUTHOR OF
> *THE SCIENCE OF MIND*

The Importance of Identifying Fears

Have you ever noticed, or practiced, this ironic human tendency? The more we want something, the more we seem likely to delay its fulfillment. Perhaps it's because there's a useful purpose to un-fulfilled goals. They serve as "if onlys," escape valves we can fan-tasize about during boring business meetings, traffic jams, and hectic mornings with the kids. We wistfully indulge in images of how great life will be once we fulfill our dreams.

Logic would dictate that if we really wanted to change our lives, we would just do it. Instead, we usually put off goals until next Monday. When Monday comes around, we reschedule the goal until some other time. We never feel quite prepared to start, always feeling a little short on money, time, or expertise.

Fears and other blocks don't usually go away by ignoring them. Blocks need to be identified and brought to light before they can be completely excised. We're not going to spend much time ana-lyzing fears, because anything you focus on for a long period will eventually increase. *We must always focus on what we want, not on what we don't want.* Instead, we will briefly identify success blocks as a way of rapidly removing them.

It's not always easy to recognize fears that block us. Many of us stubbornly insist, "I'm not afraid of anything!" But fears aren't always obvious. In fact, procrastination and the fear of failure are so powerful that they come disguised in different maladies including:

— *Overeating:* Henrietta hated doing housework, so she'd procrastinate getting the day started. She'd tell herself, "I'll clean up right after I'm done with breakfast." Then, Henrietta would eat bowl after bowl of breakfast cereal in order to delay the task as long as possible.

— *Lethargy:* "I'm too tired to exercise," "I don't feel like going out and trying to meet people tonight," "I don't have the energy to go to night school." Lethargy and lack of energy feel very real, yet they, too, are based on fears of failure.

Failure, and even the thought of failure, is extremely painful, and humans will do anything to avoid pain. One of our more ingenious avoidance mechanisms is to be too tired to start a project. We think about starting it, and our brain becomes overwhelmed. So we "turn off" our energy level and feel fatigued as a result.

The source of all energy—God—is unlimited, and we can all instantly tap into this power. You've experienced this phenomenon when someone has suddenly suggested doing something that really excites you. Suddenly, you're in the mood and raring to go.

— *Physical illness:* Becoming ill or injured is another way of avoiding the pain of failure. For example, Katrina developed a sore throat every time she planned to ask her boss for a raise.

— *Relationship problems:* Sophie blamed her husband for her unhappiness, believing a "real man" makes a huge income, buys his wife gifts, and treats the family to frequent vacations. She belittled him and complained about his meager salary, and not surprisingly, the couple's marriage started to founder. In therapy, Sophie uncovered the fears that blocked her from pursuing her own sources of income that could supplement the family budget.

The Forms of Fear

Most people who procrastinate are afraid of something, and sometimes they're not even aware what they're afraid of. Here are some of the most common fears that lead to procrastination:

— *Believing you don't deserve success.* "I have this sense that good things only happen to other people," said my client Marge. "I have dreams, but that's all they will ever be— dreams." Marge had decided that she didn't deserve to have a better life. Instead of facing possible disappointment, she decided not to even try. Over the years, I've helped thousands of childhood abuse and neglect survivors who have held this deep-seated belief.

Abuse survivors usually grow up in environments that foster negative images about themselves and about their abilities to succeed. Abusive parents—who are usually alcoholic, drug addicted, mentally ill, or temperamental—pass along their "why even try to better your life?" attitudes to their children. Some abusive parents blame their impoverished existences on their kids. Other parents verbally berate their children with derisive messages like, "You'll always fail," or "You're stupid." Little wonder these children grow up doubting their worthiness and abilities.

— *Fearing that attempts to improve one's life will only make things worse.* Cathy and her husband Bob wanted to quit their jobs and open a business. However, fear that the business would fail prevented them from even investigating the possibility.

— *Fear of being controlled.* "I don't want to be told what to do!" We often rebel against rules, even those that are self-imposed. This is one reason why diets are difficult to stick to. Sometimes, this fear of being controlled is an adulthood version of rebelling against a parent. If your folks always told you what to do, you may grow up swearing that you'll never be controlled again. This philosophy is a double-edged sword, however. While it does create an entrepreneurial spirit, it also makes self-discipline difficult.

— *Thinking you need to develop the right "contacts" to achieve success.* Anita wanted to be a talk-show host, and she clearly had the looks, personality, and intelligence to accomplish this goal. She hosted a popular public-access talk show, and lived close to Los Angeles where they film many shows. Her friends encouraged her to get an agent and a demo tape and "go for it." Yet, Anita didn't believe enough in herself to take a direct approach to her goal. Instead, she decided to take a sales job at a luxury car dealership. Although the shop was 60 miles away from Los Angeles, Melinda believed she'd develop contacts who would help her fulfill her dream. "I'll meet rich customers who'll help me get into show business," she explained to her friends.

— *Believing you don't have enough knowledge.* Jonathan, a man who attended one of my seminars, told me he'd been to dozens of workshops during the past two years. He shared his dream with me: "Someday, I want to be a motivational speaker." Jonathan explained that he was a self-made millionaire with many theories that would inspire and benefit other people. I asked him when he was going to start his speaking business. "I'm not sure," he replied. "I just don't feel ready yet."

— *Feeling too old.* "I'm too old to go to college!" complained 42-year-old Martin. "If I start now, it'd take me six years of part-time schooling to get my bachelor's degree. I'd be almost 50 years old by the time I graduated!" I reminded Martin that he'd be that same age in six years, whether he went to college or not.

— *Avoiding displeasure.* Many activities involved with goal accomplishment seem tough or monotonous. Night school, exercise, and other means of self-improvement seem like unpleasant alternatives to time spent in more leisurely pursuits. Judy's dream of being an actress helped her endure the boring hours at her secretarial job. She'd think about the accolades, the awards, and the fans' adoration. Yet every time Judy would consider enrolling in acting class, she'd decide she was too busy.

— *Fear of making a wrong decision.* "I know I'm unhappy, but I can't figure out what would make me feel better," complained my client Patty. "Sometimes I think that changing jobs would help. But then I decide that it's my husband who is driving me crazy, and I wonder about getting a divorce. At other times, I think all I need is a long vacation. I go around in circles trying to figure out what I should do!"

Fear of making a wrong decision keeps people in limbo, as they procrastinate deciding which way to go. Sure, it's a good idea to research one's options instead of just diving in. However, eternally stalling on making a decision *is* deciding to stay exactly where you are now. In addition, some people are so frightened of making a decision that they spend all their time researching their options.

— *Fear of ridicule or disapproval.* A woman I know named Martha still remembers the time when, as a little girl, she danced in a school talent show. At the end of her tap-dance, Martha looked down at her mother, expecting to receive a beaming smile. Instead, her mother was red-faced and jaw-clenched. As Martha climbed off the stage, Martha's mother began scolding her about her "poor performance," asking the little girl how she could be so cruel as to embarrass her mother in front of everyone. Little Martha never thought to question this assessment; she assumed her mother was correct. From then on, Martha was quite careful to avoid any behavior that anyone could construe as a poor performance. Consequently, Martha never pursued any dream that could possibly result in ridicule, disapproval, or embarrassment.

— *Fear of abandonment.* Sometimes we fear how others will view us if we make significant life changes. Kate was afraid that her husband would leave her if she enrolled in night school. "I know he'll be upset if I'm not home at night," she sighed. Another woman, Barbara, expressed the fear that her friends would be jealous if she lost weight. "They won't want to spend time with me if I get thinner than they are," she worried.

— *Distrusting whether you can accomplish what you set out to do.* Robin really wanted to lose weight and knew that exercise was imperative. However, she doubted that workouts would work for her. "I've spent a fortune on fitness equipment," she explained. "Nothing I do seems to work. I get hurt, sore, tired, and discouraged. Why should I even bother exercising again?"

— *Fear of being like one's parent.* Abuse survivors are especially prone to this fear, which we call "de-identification," or purposely acting the opposite of someone. Her alcoholic father had abused my client, Tamara, from age seven through nine. The experience deeply wounded her, but her mother's behavior especially enraged her. "My mother's a completely spineless wimp," Tamara told me. "She knew the abuse was going on, but she was afraid to confront my father because she thought he'd abandon us. Later, when I told her what had been going on, she accused me of bringing it on myself. As far as I'm concerned, my mother sold me out to keep a roof over our heads. I may as well have been her prostitute!"

Tamara swore she'd never be "a spineless wimp" like her mother. Now, being assertive is very healthy, of course. However, Tamara took her self-proclaimed vow to the extreme and became tough, defensive, and aggressive. This stance resulted in many problems in her love life, friendships, and career. Every time Tamara would get involved with a man, she'd be argumentative in order to "prove" her toughness and independence. She'd also argue with her bosses and co-workers for the same reason.

She worked in therapy on forgiving her mother, her father, and herself for the years of abuse. When she finally let go of years of rage and resentment, Tamara was free to decide for herself. "I'm no longer obsessing about my sexual abuse," she says. "All those years, I was so concerned about not being like mother. But I wasn't being like myself, either."

— *Thinking that there is something inherently wrong, defective, or missing in you.* "I know God made everyone perfect, in His image," my client Frank told me. "But I think He made a mistake when He made me." Many of my clients have echoed Frank's sentiments, admitting that they harbored secret fears that other people could sense they were "defective" or "unworthy." These feelings are especially prevalent among survivors of childhood abuse (including neglect).

— *The Impostor Phenomenon.* Fred had always had a nagging fear that he was unqualified for the middle-management job he held. He feared discovery and dismissal for being a fraud, a fear that kept Fred in a limbo position: he wanted to advance to upper management, but thought he had no business aspiring to such a lofty goal.

— *Fearing that things in your family will fall apart if you don't hang in there and supervise.* Candice was tired of being the bookkeeper for the family business. She dreamed of the day when she could indulge in her dream of painting pictures of angels. However, Candice thought that if she wasn't in control of the accounting books, her husband would neglect to pay taxes and fill out necessary operating forms. The family had sufficient money to hire a competent bookkeeper to take Candice's place; however, she balked. Candice finally had to confront her own fears about being dispensable. Deep down, Candice feared that if she didn't serve as protector and super-bookkeeper, her husband wouldn't appreciate her.

— *Believing that other people in your life (husband, friends, parents) first need to change before you'll succeed.* "I'd have more time if my friends didn't stop by the house all the time," complained my client Judy. "It just seems like all my friends want to tell me about their problems." Judy explained that she was postponing her dream of writing children's books until the day when her friends were stable and less dependent upon her for help. "Then I won't feel guilty taking time for my own goals," she added.

— *Fearing change.* Allison had lived alone her entire adult life. Although she dreamed of being married and having a family, Allison wasn't sure whether she could accept another person's presence in her home life.

— *Believing that unhappiness, fear, and guilt are requisite human states.* A common, but deep-seated, belief that keeps us from improving our lives is the sense that, "I must endure emotional pain before I'll be allowed to feel happiness." We almost act as if we must collect a certain amount of sadness, fear, and guilt like trading stamps so we can redeem them for the feelings of peace, security, love, and happiness we crave.

— *Feeling unprepared.* "I really want to be an actress," my client Regina told me. "But first I need to take another drama class." I pointed out to Regina that she'd taken five years of classes and suggested that perhaps she was merely postponing the pursuit of her dream. She committed to stop preparing and to, instead, start pursuing her dream. Three months later, Regina had an agent, was auditioning, and said she felt energized by her new activities.

You Deserve Success

"There is only one corner of the universe you can be certain of improving, and that's your own self."
— ALDOUS HUXLEY (1894–1963),
ENGLISH AUTHOR/PHILOSOPHER

Let's look at success blocks just a bit more, to ensure that no hidden fears thwart your desires. We're not going to overanalyze these fears—that would only amplify them, since whatever we focus upon always increases. Instead of focusing on fear, we're merely *moving* the fear out of the darkness. We're coaxing fear out into daylight where it will pop like a soap bubble warmed by the sun. Then we'll see your true, natural fear-free self.

✦ ✦ ✦

Deservingness: Of all the blocks to success—whether in career, love, or health—this is the biggest and most destructive. If you don't believe you deserve success, you push it away. The deservingness issue seems illogical. Who doesn't want success, after all? Yet, *wanting* success is different from *believing* you can have it. A person may want a better job, for example, but think, "Yeah, right! Dream on!" So, this individual doesn't even try.

If you doubt that you deserve success, it's the equivalent of deciding that you will fail. You'll anticipate failure, resulting in a self-fulfilling prophecy. However, when you know that you—like everyone else—deserve success, you graciously accept good as it comes to you. You enjoy compliments, gifts, and job promotions. You also generously give to others. Deservingness means knowing that giving and receiving are natural parts of life. Good is welcomed, not feared.

Many of my clients, particularly abuse and neglect survivors, have felt undeserving of success. "Other people deserve success, but not me." Usually, this feeling stems from years of self-blame with respect to the abuse: "I must be a very bad child for Daddy to treat me this way, or for Mommy to be so mad at me."

Although her parents had not physically abused my client Tina, the neglect and verbal abuse she grew up with had convinced her that she was "no good" and didn't deserve success. Aspiring to be an artist, Tina had taken many art classes and painted beautiful portraits that graced her living room and office. When a friend suggested that Tina show her art in the neighborhood art show, Tina panicked. She didn't feel that she was good enough to have an art show, so she protested, "I don't have time to create enough paintings!"

Now Tina had always dreamed of being a professional artist. In fact, her favorite dream was of a San Francisco gallery where her art was showing. In this fantasy, Tina gracefully waltzed around the room chatting with appreciative art patrons. She saw herself in a chic silk pantsuit, happily socializing with champagne-sipping men and women who oozed compliments about her creations.

This dream injected Tina's drearier days with color and hope. It fueled her and lent her an escape into a world of her own, where she felt appreciated and in control. The only trouble was that *Tina never expected the dream to come true*. She said, "I wish this fantasy would come true, but I really don't see how it could happen. I believe I have talent, and I'll often look at other artists' work and say, 'I could paint something even better than that.' I just feel my work is undeveloped. I don't paint much, so there's no way for me to improve my abilities. I fantasize about running away to a deserted island with a palette and a paintbrush—someplace where no one would bug me and where I could just paint all day."

When Tina and I talked further, I realized that undeservingness was apparently at the heart of her "detached dreaming"—that is, her belief that she couldn't accomplish her goals. Tina felt that other people deserved good, but not her. She described a belief that successful artists were people who were "different" than she was. Tina even surprised herself when acknowledging her misconception that all successful artists were lucky, well connected, beautiful, or supremely talented. "I know better than to hold a belief like this!" she told me. "I know the power of thought, yet here I am sabotaging myself with my own thinking."

We uncovered and treated the two sources of her undeservingness: verbal abuse and neglect in childhood; and self-abuse as an adult. Tina's mother had told her that she could never make it as an artist because she was "uncoordinated, lazy, and had no talent at all." As with most children, Tina incorporated her mother's cruel words into her self-image. Tina believed that she was lazy and untalented; therefore, she acted that way. When she grew up, Tina's harsh attitudes about herself hardened even more. Tina wouldn't even start anything new, like an exercise program, a relationship, or an art career. "Why should I even bother? I'll just screw everything up or end up quitting, anyway," she'd affirm.

Our therapy consisted of rescripting Tina's self-image with words that truly matched her God-given self: unlimited energy, talent, creativity, love, health, and abundance. We used many of the methods described in this book. Within a short amount of time, Tina's life improved in every way: her love life blossomed, she lost weight, and she had an art showing at a major gallery!

Feeling Damaged

Another block to success is feeling damaged, as if something is inherently wrong with you:

"I know that God made everybody else perfect, but I think He made a mistake with me."

So many clients have expressed this sentiment to me! As with other fears, survivors of childhood neglect or abuse are more apt to think this way than those raised in love and harmony.

Many people who were abused growing up don't understand, trust, or expect loving behavior. All they've ever known is criticism, neglect, and cruelty. So is it any wonder that they continue to abuse themselves as adults? They have come to view pain as normal and to view kindness with suspicion.

Self-punishment is a product of guilt. There's a sense that, "I'm bad and I deserve punishment." This guilt stems from a vague notion that deep inside, one is defective and unworthy. The person may connect this feeling with a specific deed, or it could be a general belief that "I'm a bad person, and everybody who meets me knows it."

Self-punishment takes many different forms:

1. *Putting oneself last.* Maria complained that her family responsibilities took so much time and energy that she couldn't exercise. Throughout her life, Maria had put her own needs last.

   On closer examination of her schedule, however, we found that Maria spent an inordinate number of hours cleaning her preteen children's rooms and clothes. So we placed her sons and daughter on a chore and allowance schedule, which gave Maria time to go to the gym.

2. *Not setting, starting, or completing goals.* Daniel was unhappy and lonely. He wanted a love relationship, but instead, he put off this goal. Daniel would tell himself, "I'll join a dating club after I lose weight," or "What's the use? There aren't any decent single women." These self-defeating beliefs were Daniel's way of protecting himself against fears of rejection by women.

   We worked to unravel Daniel's negative beliefs and to set realistic "love goals." First, he listed all the characteristics that were important to him in a love relationship and partner. Next, he pushed himself to leave the house at night so he could meet eligible partners. Daniel attended adult education courses, seminars, and a spiritual study group. Within two months, Daniel met and began dating a woman who truly sparked his romantic interests.

3. *Being a martyr/victim.* Rebecca was big on volunteering for charitable, civic, and school district projects. She passionately believed that citizens should give freely of their time and other resources. All this would be fine, but Rebecca now found herself serving on so many committees that she complained of being overwhelmed with responsibilities. She was usually irritable because she felt victimized by the organizations she was volunteering for.

Rebecca had accepted the role of "Martyr/Victim"—that is, someone who is the long-suffering and virtuous victim of other people's uncaring manipulations. She didn't see how she played any part in defining her role. All she saw was a good-girl/bad-world dichotomy.

4. *Squandering resources.* Kathleen's goal was to pay off her credit cards, yet each weekend, she'd charge purchases of new clothes or household items. Frank wanted to finish his M.B.A. degree through the correspondence course in which he'd enrolled. However, Frank spent his spare time watching television instead of completing his homework assignments. Both Kathleen and Frank complained that outside sources interfered with their goals, while in truth they were singly responsible for sabotaging their own success.

5. *Staying in unhealthy relationships.* Trina and her boyfriend Mark had been dating for two years. She was unhappy because Mark had had two affairs of which she was aware. He also verbally mistreated her. Still, Trina felt that she could change Mark by loving him more than any other woman. In therapy, Trina discovered that her desire to win Mark's love stemmed from her unfulfilled relationship with her father, who deserted the family when she was five years old.

6. *Negative self-talk.* Donna wanted to have more confidence and self-assurance at work. In therapy, we discovered her propensity for negative self-talk: "You'll always mess up," "You're stupid; nobody will listen to you," and so on. Through affirmations, Donna adopted an outlook that made her feel and act more confident.

7. *Mistreatment of one's body.* Barbara pushed her body into action every day by consuming stimulants such as coffee, colas,

and chocolate bars. At night, Barbara would feel jittery as a result of her stress-inducing diet. So, she'd drink a bottle of wine to fall asleep.

8. *Being stingy with oneself* (not buying treats or even essentials; not seeing a dentist or doctor as needed; driving with a cracked windshield).

9. *Trying too hard to please others.* More than anything, Brenda wanted to be liked and accepted by her co-workers. Her method for attracting their friendship was costing Brenda her own self-respect, however. She would often pick up the tab for their lunches, or offer to complete her co-worker's job duties. The women that Brenda worked with always said yes to her offers to pay or to help. Still, Brenda noticed that they never reciprocated her generosity. She wondered what it was about her that people didn't like. She was so good to everybody and tried hard not to make them angry or get in their way. It seemed to her that the more she tried to be liked, the less people seemed to notice her.

Self-punishment is akin to paying penance. The belief is that self-destruction will relieve feelings of guilt. It's the thought, "If I'm punished for doing wrong, then I won't feel so bad." Unfortunately, self-punishment only amplifies feelings of unworthiness for "inner-child abusers."

As it says in *A Course in Miracles*, "Love and guilt cannot co-exist, and to choose one is to deny the other." Take Stephanie, for example:

As a single mother of two young children and a full-time loan officer, Stephanie's days practically zoomed by. Between working, shopping, shuttling the kids around, and keeping the house clean, she had little free time.

Stephanie craved relaxation and play time, and she also dreamed of meeting and marrying a good man. But every time Stephanie went on a date, her children would scream protests over being left with a babysitter. The guilt of leaving her children would ruin Stephanie's moods, and she often left dates early to return home. She wondered whether she'd have to wait until her children were grown before resuming a social life.

The Impostor Phenomenon

At age 33, Joseph was the youngest manager at his corporation. His rise to the top had been swift. Of course, success had always come easily to the youngest son of a well-educated New England family.

Joseph secretly wondered if he deserved the gifts life had bestowed upon him. In therapy, he shared his fear that "my bosses will discover I'm a fake and that I'm really not very good at what I do. Actually, my secretary and assistant do most of the thinking, planning, and working that I get paid to do. I feel like someday, someone will blow the whistle on me, and then I'll be out on my ear!"

Joseph was suffering from "The Impostor Phenomenon," the feeling that one is actually an undeserving charlatan of sorts. This syndrome is extremely common among successful people, but usually, once they have acknowledged these feelings, they let go of the false beliefs. Believing that one is an impostor doesn't mean that someone *is* an impostor.

People like Joseph who fear being "found out" are simply discounting their talents and abilities because it seems that success came without any kind of struggle. Joseph said he felt guilty about easily getting "A's" in college while his brothers struggled to make passing grades. Yet in truth, Joseph earned his scholastic merit through his own system of hard work: taking excellent notes in class, concentrated study of his textbooks, and maintaining a calm and positive attitude while taking tests.

Joseph had always pushed himself to focus on the next mountain to climb, instead of resting and appreciating how far he'd already come. He feared becoming complacent if he took stock of his progress. His insecurity was both his driving motivational force and the root of his feelings of inadequacy. When I encouraged Joseph to take credit for his intense focus and superb studying skills, he smiled and said, "Yes, I guess I really have worked hard to get where I am."

"Really, It Doesn't Bother Me!"

Rationalizations are little prisons of the mind that enable us to cope with unacceptable situations. I once visited a man in jail, and I asked how he was coping with his lack of freedom. He said, "You know, I really could kick my way out of this prison cell if I put my mind to it." I took a quick breath at the outrageousness of his statement, but then realized that this thought was his way of staying sane. He had convinced himself that he was *choosing* to stay incarcerated.

How often have we used the same type of thinking to put up with unacceptable behavior in others, or to remain in an unfulfilling job?

I remember one client who worked in a factory. She detested her job, with its noise, filth, and foul-mouthed co-workers. Practically every therapy session involved complaints about her work environment. One day I finally asked her if she'd considered changing to another occupation. My question startled her. "Well, in only 12 more years I can retire!" was her reply.

To her, 12 years seemed like a bargain in exchange for the attractive retirement package the company promised her. To me, it seemed unfathomable, since I view 12 years as a very substantial chunk of time.

Waiting for Permission

Many people procrastinate making life changes because of fears of disapproval from others. I've also worked with many clients who state that they're waiting for some authority figure to give them *permission* or the go-ahead to change their lives.

> Helen wanted to divorce her verbally abusive husband, Dave, but she was afraid her parents would criticize her for being a "failure." Helen and Dave had separated three times, and each time he swore he'd get counseling and be more loving. They would reconcile, and Dave would soon start to belittle and ridicule his wife.
>
> Although Helen wanted out of her painful marriage, the thought of her family's scorn petrified her. Desperately wanting her family's permission to divorce Dave, Helen openly complained about her husband's behavior. She told her father about Dave's put-downs, but her parents did not voice the words she waited to hear: "We think you should divorce Dave, Helen."

Many people such as Helen have internalized their parents' voices and can almost hear the sound of their mother saying, "Do this," or "Don't do that." Those raised in abusive households often feel paralyzed by the fear of making a mistake. While growing up, Helen's angry parents often demanded to know why she had been bad. Helen had tried *so hard* to be good; she couldn't imagine what she had done wrong! Often, alcohol unduly influenced her parents when they decided she was "a bad girl" for some reason.

Helen waited for some external force to prompt her to start her goals. She described the expectation that some authority figure was going to tap her on the shoulder and say, "Okay, it's time to start living the life you really want."

This is a common feeling, one that stems from childhood, where parents dictate when and what we do. As children, we receive praise for following orders. As adults, we find ourselves in dead-end jobs and unhealthy relationships in the same way. To survive as children, we must give away some of our control. The irony is that giving away control as an adult is averse to states of well-being and health.

Self-Fulfilling Fears

Fears interfere with success and soul growth when they paralyze us into catatonic procrastination. But fears inflict far deeper wounds if they manifest themselves into living nightmares, as you'll read:

A neighbor of mine named Melissa was a 41-year-old administrator and single parent of a young daughter. She was so proud the day that she purchased her oceanfront condominium. She was the first in her family to own real estate, and the fact that she bought it without financial aid from a husband or parent made her a role model for her female friends.

When Melissa moved in to her new home, however, she started feeling paranoid that she'd lose her beloved condominium. She relished the sea air wafting into her kitchen, yet she couldn't enjoy it. Melissa worried about losing her job and being unable to meet the mortgage payments. Once or twice a week, Melissa had nightmares of having the condominium foreclosed.

Her fears became obsessive, and she dwelled on them continually. Melissa consulted psychics to foresee possible financial problems. Each psychic assured Melissa that there was nothing to worry about, and one even warned her that fears can turn into reality. Still, Melissa felt a form of the Impostor Phenomenon, believing that she didn't deserve to maintain such a wonderful lifestyle.

Melissa's insomnia and incessant worrying affected her immune system, resulting in a serious case of pneumonia. She took time off from her job, which caused even more financial worries. Given all the stress, Melissa's illness lingered for several months, and she did lose her job. She was beside herself! Now she was certain to lose her condo! For the next year, Melissa's frantic state made for poor job interviews, and she couldn't find a new position. Her savings account dried up, and the bank foreclosed her home two years after she'd bought it.

The crisis brought Melissa to her knees. She wanted to understand what had happened to her. Had she brought it on herself, or was life just simply unfair? Melissa had no money or insurance for counseling, so she joined a free women's support group offered by the county. In this nurturing environment, Melissa came to understand that her fears had manifested into illness and inactivity on her part. Today, she is using a proactive plan to focus her mind and emotions on what she *does* want, not on what she doesn't want.

I feel that Melissa's prognosis for rebuilding her life is wonderful, and this time, she'll know how to build, instead of destroy, her dreams.

The Woman Who Had No Time for Cancer

Another woman discovered the power of fears and decisions in a near-fatal way.

Anna Maria, the successful owner of a San Francisco spa, has always been sensitive to the positive and nega-

tive energies of the world. "Being around positive people
is an inspiration, and validation for what I want in my life.
Being around negative people is invalidating," she explains. "I love the burst of energy I get when I read something positive or watch the Olympics."

Yet, for all that positive energy, Anna Maria once harbored some powerful fears. Her aunt had died of breast
cancer, and Anna Maria was deeply afraid of suffering the
same fate. She became very active in running breast cancer fund raisers, and she immersed herself in learning
about the disease.

In 1987, her worst fears were realized, and doctors di-
agnosed her with breast cancer. Anna Maria recalled what
happened next, "You get what you fear the most, and I really feared breast cancer. I feel like I attracted it to me. I
knew that at the time, and I was angry with myself for
doing this. For one thing, I had too many things going on
in my life, and I didn't want to be sick. I remember being
wheeled in on a gurney when I decided, 'I don't have
TIME for this!'" Soon after deciding that she had no time
for cancer, Anna Maria went into remission. Today, she
guards her thoughts carefully to ensure that she will only
attract what she wants into her life.

The Universal Law of Attraction declares that what we think
about forms the basis for our experiences in life. You are deciding
today what you want your life to be like tomorrow. My publisher,
Louise Hay, says that our life today is a product of what we thought
six months ago.

Such power, once acknowledged, is both frightening and exciting. It's the realization that you can have whatever you decide upon,
and only your beliefs and judgments hold you back. Look for fears
and limiting beliefs as you'd seek weeds in a garden. Observe them,

and then yank them out by the root! I hope you'll choose some wonderful dreams. *You deserve them.*

From Fear to Fearlessness

We are briefly examining fears so they can vanish. This is different from two other unhealthy and ineffective means of dealing with fears: overanalyzing them, which increases the fear; or denying them, which causes fear to block success from a hidden vantage point.

Notice your fear without judging it as either "bad" or "good." Simply tell yourself, "Aha, I notice I am feeling afraid." When we judge our fears as bad, we feel more afraid, like we messed up. However, a detached observation of a fear allows you to discard the fear without expecting a slap on the wrist for making a mistake. While fear is rooted in mistaken thoughts about yourself and others, it only requires correction, not punishment. Correct your thoughts so they revert back to the truth that you, and everyone else, is perfect, whole, and complete. Ask for spiritual support if this step seems difficult. Correct your thoughts, and you'll find that the fear—which was an effect of your mistaken thinking—will be forgotten.

Whenever you feel fear, say to yourself, "I am noticing I am afraid. I am observing this fear, without being consumed by the fear. I am asking my inner self to tell me what important information or lesson is contained within this fear."

Everyone feels afraid from time to time, and this is not an appeal for you to attain some impossible ideal. That would be a form of denial! Please know, however, how much power you have within you to get rid of fear once you notice its presence in your thoughts. *Know* that you can learn to trust your inner guide to keep you safe from all fears and worries.

Fears learned in childhood stem from being small and dependent. But today, you can choose to lose those fears, and decide upon your own destiny. If you are in danger, your inner guide and angels will warn you. Meanwhile, *go for it,* and move toward your dreams today!

There Is Nothing to Fear

If we remove fear from our lives, then all things become possible.

Think about it, and see if you agree: if you had a strong, clear desire and held no fears or doubts, nothing would be standing in your way. You would simply act responsibly, intelligently, and consistently toward the fulfillment and accomplishment of your goals, correct? You would also have more energy, since fear drains enthusiasm like a vampire.

However, fears are painful. Instead of facing them, we use lack of time as an excuse. We also become trapped in cycles that really do erode the amount of available time and energy we have—cycles such as staying in emotionally and spiritually toxic jobs or relationships, being exhausted or dispirited because we have spent ten hours working at a meaningless job, and engaging in hours of telephone conversations complaining that we're not getting anywhere in life.

If you had no fear of failure, what would you dream?

By the time you've finished this book, this question will seem backwards and almost humorous to you! Because, fear is exactly *why* you haven't realized your dreams to date. These fears keep you from asking the universe and other people to help you realize your dreams. Once you *ask* to have your needs met, they *will* be met. It's just scary to ask for what you want.

When you really want something, you always make time to ensure it happens. You just do it! The same is true for all your current goals. Once you identify and remove your fears, you will find and make the time to accomplish whatever it is you want. You simply won't let anything or anybody stand in your way!

POINTS TO REMEMBER

❧ Procrastination stems from fear and indecision.

❧ When you really want something, you always find and make time for its accomplishment. Once we remove fear and indecision, we have more time to fulfill desires.

❧ The Impostor Phenomenon is a common malady among successful people who secretly fear being "discovered" as frauds who haven't earned their stature.

❧ Not only do fears interfere with goal attainment, but they can also be self-fulfilling. Fear and worry cause more falls than they prevent.

❧ It's important to identify fears and success blocks as a first step in removing them. Identify, but don't overanalyze, your fears. Remember: think about what you want, rather than what you don't want.

❧ Observe and notice fears, without judging them.

❧ Fears are normal. However, removing fear is both a healthy and attainable goal. When we remove fear, all things become possible.

CHAPTER SIX

STORIES OF CONQUERING TIME AND FEAR

"I must govern the clock, not be governed by it."
— GOLDA MEIR (1898–1978), ISRAELI
PRIME MINISTER

Many people hold sweeping beliefs about "the way things are." For example, "Women never get ahead," "Companies would never promote me because of my ethnicity," "My parents put too many negative messages into my head; I'll always be hampered by them," or "I don't have a college degree, so I can't possibly succeed."

These beliefs become self-fulfilling, because you think you've lost the race before it even begins. You don't even bother trying, or you put in a halfhearted effort.

Here are some success stories to help banish such absolute statements.

— *Limiting Belief #1*: "How can I get ahead when I've got little children to raise?"

Do you think your children or spouse block you? Lose this limiting belief, and you'll clear the way to success, as did Dottie Walters:

After high school, Dottie's friends all went away to college. She felt very alone, until the realization hit her: *No one is going to help me go to college. I'm all alone.* Dottie threw herself into reading autobiographies, and her favorite was about Amelia Earhart. One phrase voiced by the female pilot particularly inspired her, and she still carries these words in her wallet:

> *"Some of us have great runways already built for us. If you do, USE IT and take off! If you don't have a runway, you must build one of your own."*

Dottie went to college, got married, and had two children. Still, she was unhappy because she and her husband struggled to pay their bills. Dottie was tired of living in poverty! At first, she resented her husband for his low earnings. Of course, her resentment didn't improve a thing. "Finally," she recalls, "I surrendered. I said to myself, 'Okay, I accept responsibility. If I want to better my financial situation, I need to take steps myself.'"

Recalling her lifelong ambition to write professionally, Dottie went to the local newspaper office with both babies in tow. Outside the building, a large sign read, "NO HELP WANTED." Unfazed, Dottie went in anyway and adamantly asked to see the publisher.

In the waiting area, Dottie decided that if the newspaper was low on cash, she would pay for the space of printing her column. She planned to write about local businesses and restaurants, charging the merchants a fee to have information about their business appear in print.

Face to face with the harried publisher, Dottie explained her proposal. "I have a very interesting column I want you to use," she told him. "I will pay you for the space at wholesale and then sell it at retail." Then, rather than asking him for an okay, Dottie gave the publisher two op-

tions: "Would you rather that I pay you for the first column in two weeks or in three weeks?"

He answered, "Three weeks," which was fortunate considering that Dottie was penniless and needed the extra
time to convince merchants to pay her.

Dottie worked at home while caring for her family. Her
business rapidly grew. Soon, she employed 285 people in
four offices, and had 4,000 contract advertising accounts. Today, Dottie Walters runs a successful speaker's
bureau, is the author of *Speak and Grow Rich*, and pub-
lishes a speaker's trade magazine. She lives by her motto:
"Don't postpone your success—do it now!"

— *Limiting Belief #2*: "Women are never promoted, so why
should I even try?"

Do you think being a woman holds you back? Lose this belief, so you can experience limitless joy, as did Patricia
Jethalal:

Anyone who has moved to another city or state can appreciate the courage it took for young Pat Jethalal to
move, all by herself, from her native South Africa to the
United States. In need of money and having heard that
American salespeople had unlimited incomes, Pat decided
to sell insurance. At the time, there were very few female
insurance agents.

Pat's male peers resented working with a woman, and
none would help train her for her new job. The only way
Pat could receive training was to pay any man who would
take her on a sales appointment 50 percent of her commission. Nevertheless, she knew that in the end, she'd
come out on top. She did!

Today, Pat is a general manager for one of the world's
top insurance agencies, where 55 male and female agents

work for her. She is one of the most successful women agents in the country, earns a great salary, and has won many industry awards.

Pat told me the philosophy by which she lives and works: "You can be successful if you have a passion. Commit to your dreams, and *stick* to them. Stay focused. You can achieve anything you want, and it doesn't matter if you are a man or a woman."

— *Limiting Belief #3:* "I can't get ahead without a college degree, so I may as well stick with my present job."
Do you believe a lack of education holds you back? Lose that belief, and you'll enjoy more opportunities, as did Ruth Ko:

Raven-haired Ruth, a high school dropout, turned her love of dance into a profession. First, she hula danced with Don Ho's troupe. She later worked as a Tahitian dancer at the Disneyland Tiki Hut room. However, Ruth longed for more meaningful work and a salary that would allow her to completely pay the mortgage on her home. So she took an advertising sales job at a weekly shopping magazine. Ruth worked hard, became the manager, and later the general manager. Everything seemed great, until the publishers announced that the magazine was up for sale.

Ruth worried about whether the new publisher would keep her at her position and salary. She figured that there was only one way to ensure her continual employment: buy the magazine herself! To purchase the magazine, Ruth would need to be the top bidder in a competitive buying situation. She calculated that $650,000 would be a successful bid, so Ruth took a deep breath along with her life savings, and added a second mortgage to her home.

The only other bidder was a man who took one look at Ruth and figured she would bid considerably too low. He underestimated her, though! She submitted the winning bid, and today Ruth Ko is the owner of one of the most successful regional magazines in the country. With advertising revenues nearing $3.2 million, Ruth achieved her dual goal of attaining meaningful work and paying off the mortgages on her home.

— *Limiting Belief #4*: "The business world is prejudiced against people of my race or ethnicity. The only way I'll move ahead is if I get a lucky break!"

Do you believe your race, ethnic group, creed, or religion interferes with attaining your goals? Lose that belief to reveal the paths that will lead you to more enjoyment and fulfillment, as did Marty Rodriguez:

Marty was the fourth of eleven children in a poor Hispanic household in Southern California. At age 12, Marty cleaned houses and ironed clothes after school to help pay for food, shelter, and clothing. Frequently, she and her mother arrived at a new housecleaning client's home, only to be turned away because the homeowner didn't want Hispanics inside the house.

Today, though, homeowners welcome Marty! She's now top salesperson among both men and women *in the world* for Century 21 Real Estate, a title she has earned for three successive years. In the sluggish real estate market of Los Angeles County, during the worst recession in years, Marty sold more than 1,200 homes in ten years and netted over six million dollars. In 1993, the slowest sales year in recent real estate history, Marty sold 173 homes and earned almost one-and-a-quarter million dollars. How did she manage to shatter all records and beat incredible odds to fulfill her dreams and aspirations? Largely through The Universal Law of Responsibility, as you will see.

As a child, Marty competed with herself to be best at everything, simply because it felt so good to be the best. As an adult, Marty became a successful real estate agent by applying her lifelong work ethic of rising to the top. During the real estate boom in the 1980s, houses practically sold themselves. Then the recession of the 1990s hit, and the real estate market dropped to a trickle.

Marty decided to stay in real estate. She loved selling houses, and the recession had hurt her husband's contracting business. They needed the money! The answer was clear: instead of buckling under to the economic slowdown, Marty would have to buckle down and get to work!

Marty cleared her schedule so she could exclusively focus on listing and selling homes. She also hired a housekeeper. Although she could barely afford this luxury initially, the extra help turned out to be the best investment Marty ever made toward career success. She often brought her children to work so they would understand and support Mommy's efforts to make a better life for the family.

Marty could have given up when the real estate market took a turn for the worse. She had every excuse for failure available to her. Marty could have said, "I'm a woman, I'm a mother, I'm a wife, I'm Hispanic, I'm from a poor family," or any other rationalization for not taking charge of her life. However, Marty doesn't see herself as a victim, and never intends to. "I don't accept any limitations at all," she says. "Your life is whatever you decide it's going to be."

Marty Rodriguez, three-time world sales leader for Century 21 Real Estate, understands that we are completely responsible for everything in our lives. Whatever shape you and your life are in right now—good, bad, or indifferent—it is because you chose and allowed it to be this way. This is not a condemnation or attempt to blame anyone for their life difficulties. It is a joyful revelation that you can script almost everything in your life.

— *Limiting Belief #5:* "I need to know the right people in order to get ahead."

    Do you believe success comes only to the well connected? Lose that belief, and enjoy the unlimited possibilities that one person can enjoy, as did Vicki Lansky:

Vicki Lansky and her husband moved from Boston, where they'd always lived, to Michigan, for his new job. Vicki was pregnant with their first child. She'd never really worked, and it didn't occur to her that she'd ever be responsible for paying any bills.

However, the *very* day before her baby was due, Vicki's husband lost his job! How would they make the house payment? Many women in Vicki's shoes would have given up and said, "What's the use? Let's just sell the house and move back with our parents."

However, Vicki resolved to make enough money to support her family and pay the mortgage. She didn't know exactly *how* she would get the money. All she knew was that she *would* get it!

"Why not make and sell a cookbook of homemade baby food recipes?"Vicki asked herself. After all, she'd recently watched her church group make money selling recipe collections. So, on a shoestring publishing budget, Vicki printed 1,000 copies of her baby-food cookbook.

The cookbooks sat in the garage until Vicki's husband urged her to get publicity. She halfheartedly gave a copy to the local newspaper food editor. Good thing she did—he praised the cookbook in his column. The next week, Vicki received 150 cookbook orders. This encouraged her to keep publicizing the book, and she eventually sold more than 100,000 self-published copies!

Vicki then sold the book to Bantam Publishers and went on a book publicity tour. The week after she appeared on the Phil Donahue show, Vicki's book, *Feed Me, I'm Yours*, was number one on the *New York Times* bestseller list. To date, *Feed Me, I'm Yours* has sold more than two million copies, and Vicki has sold more than four million copies of all her books combined.

Vicki Lansky's faith and determination helped her achieve a miracle. She saved her house from foreclosure, and her books helped millions of parents. When crises loomed in front of her, Vicki stood up to the challenge. She told herself, "If it's going to be, it's up to me."

You Are Successful, Now

You may not realize it, but you already create, set, and achieve goals every minute of the day. Take grocery shopping, for example. You write down the foods, condiments, and ingredients you want to buy. Then you drive to the supermarket, put the items from your list into your shopping cart, pay for them, and drive home.

We take this process for granted. As we make a grocery list, we never worry, "What if I can't get the items on the list? Maybe I'm not educated enough, smart enough, or thin enough!" Of course not! We just go to the grocery store and purchase the items. Why do we think other goals are any different?

It's like walking on a wooden board that lays flat on the ground. We're unafraid to walk the length of the board, because we know we can't fall. With the same wooden board suspended one inch above the ground, we would still walk its length with confidence. If we progressively raised the board higher, it would eventually reach a height that would elicit fear and trepidation. It would still be the same board, but we would be afraid of falling from it.

That outermost point where you first start to feel afraid is the edge of whatever makes you feel safe and secure. You may not be *happy* with, for example, your marriage, household routines, or your job—but they are familiar and predictable. They are like the wooden board on the ground, and you know you won't fall from them. For example:

> Karen didn't like her relationship with her unambitious, sullen boyfriend, but at least she knew he'd never leave her for another woman. Karen feared that a man who met her ideal expectations might eventually desert her.
>
> Curt didn't enjoy his dead-end job as a department store cashier, but at least he knew his job was secure. He dreamed of owning his own auto parts store, but feared the pitfalls of business ownership.

Karen and Curt were both afraid to leave the safe cocoon of familiarity. This would not be a problem if not for the fact that both were *deeply* unhappy! There's nothing wrong with feeling safe and secure. Problems arise when your comfortable life is markedly different from the life you desire.

Shaking It Up a Bit—Leaving Your Safety Cage

> *"When one door of happiness closes, another opens;*
> *but often we look so long at the closed door that we do*
> *not see the one which has been opened for us."*
> — HELEN KELLER (1880–1968)

Have you ever seen those glass-domed paperweights, the kind you shake to create snow flurries around little plastic people and houses? As you think about making your dreams a reality, you may feel your world shaking like the insides of that paperweight. I'm asking you to stretch your thoughts and faith a bit. It's a little like starting a new exercise program, where your muscles feel sore at first.

Break your cocoon barriers, so you can transform from a caterpillar into a butterfly. How? By declaring complete responsibility for being in your cocoon, and total responsibility for leaving. We become trapped when we avoid taking responsibility for the conditions in our lives. We're trapped further by blaming others for lack of fulfillment, success, and happiness.

Carrie blamed her African-American heritage for her dismal finances. Ron blamed his out-of-control drinking on his abusive father. Jan blamed her unemployed husband for her shoddy living conditions. Aaron blamed his young children for costing him so much money that he was afraid to change jobs for fear of financial loss.

By blaming other people, Carrie, Ron, Jan, and Aaron avoided taking charge of their present-day problems. Many people blame others instead of shouldering the responsibility to change their lives. Blamers are even applauded and pitied for being poor victims of circumstances.

However, does that applause or pity feel good? Is it enough to sustain you or fulfill you? Pity doesn't pay the bills or buy a better house, car, or wardrobe! Doesn't it feel better to do what you know you need to do?

Tap Yourself on the Shoulder!

If you don't like something in your life, only one person can change it: YOU! Is that good news or frightening news to you? It really is good news, because it gives you all the power you need to make necessary changes. Tap yourself on the shoulder right now, and give yourself permission to make changes.

94

All goals, dreams, wishes, and hopes are exactly like the grocery shopping list we discussed earlier. You list what you want and then go out and get it! Accepting responsibility for success and failure is not a burden, but rather, a freeing revelation. Studies show that stress stems from feeling that you are not in control of your time and your life. For example, secretaries have among the highest stress levels of employees anywhere, because they have little control over how their time is spent. Other people—bosses, co-workers and customers—are constantly interrupting the secretary and asking her to stop what's she's doing in order to perform some new task. She is stressed because she has little control or say-so about her agenda.

The word *control* has some negative connotations. However, there are two types of control—one healthy and one unhealthy. The unhealthy type of control is the one we commonly think of as negative, involving bossing-around or manipulating people, places, and things.

> For example, Helene wanted desperately to get her husband to change his drinking habits. She tried everything—complaining, dressing seductively, and urging him to attend Alcoholics Anonymous meetings—but nothing worked. Helene was trying to control something that no one but her husband could control.

Unhealthy control creates stress, both for the controlling person and everyone around him or her. Some people try to control their upsetting emotions by controlling other people. This is unhealthy because it creates relationship problems. Brad's story is typical, unfortunately, of people who engage in this type of unhealthy control:

> Brad was deeply afraid that his wife Ella would leave him for another man. He tried to control his painful jealousy and fears of abandonment indirectly, by maintaining

vigilant control over Ella's schedule. If she were even ten minutes late, Brad would unleash a verbal litany of accusations.

Healthy control focuses on what you *can* change. You *can* control your finances, your choice of lovers, your living conditions, your career choice, your education level, your weight, your circle of friends...and your schedule. When you focus on controlling these important life circumstances, you are operating under the Universal Law of Responsibility. You are now in the driver's seat of your own car, obeying the natural forces around you.

By taking complete responsibility for your life, you are, in essence, putting the key into the ignition of your life, starting your engine, and stepping on the gas! Isn't that exciting? This essential step puts the ignition key into your hands: right now, declare your responsibility for every condition—good or bad—in your life. This is a first step in dramatically changing your life for the better. For example:

— If you are in debt, accept responsibility that you chose to use (or allowed someone else to use) credit for whatever purpose, well founded or not.

— If you are overweight or out-of-shape, accept responsibility that you have eaten too much or not exercised enough.

— If your career is stalled, accept responsibility for mistaken decisions, procrastinating your education, or delays in deciding about career options.

— If your schedule is overbooked with meaningless chores or duties, accept responsibility for saying "yes" when you wanted to say "no."

— If you are unhappy in your love life, accept responsibility for the choices you have made in lovers and mates, or for the fact that you have not clearly expressed what behaviors you will and won't accept.

— If negative people surround you, accept responsibility for attracting these friends or co-workers into your life, or for agreeing to participate in the negative relationship.

— If you are unhealthy, accept responsibility for whatever lifestyle choices or thoughts may have contributed to or exacerbated your condition.

Once you have exposed yourself to the clear, bright light of accepting responsibility for your positive and negative choices, you can progress, and choose better next time. That's the good news! Since no other person is to blame for your present or past life, then no one can stop you from changing your life for the better. You were always, and will always be, in control of your life!

If this principle upsets you, it's best to examine your underlying beliefs and emotions. Ask yourself, "What purpose does it serve to remain angry, bitter, or resentful toward someone else?" Does that anger move you closer to your goals, or does it push you away from them? Most likely, the anger moves you away from purposeful efforts toward your goals. The anger is, therefore, impeding and hurting YOU! Forgive yourself and everyone you had blamed. Let it go, now.

Although Marcus had divorced Tisha four years earlier, she still felt bitter whenever she thought about him. Their child-custody battle had cost Tisha thousands of dollars and many nights of worry and anguish. For four years, she felt upset and drained whenever Marcus took their son for visitations. "If it wasn't for Marcus being in my life, *then* I would have the emotional strength to get on with my career!" was Tisha's deepest belief.

Fortunately, Tisha realized during therapy that Marcus wasn't going to disappear from her life suddenly. Tisha decided that her anger was eroding her valuable time and self-confidence. Instead of focusing on Marcus, Tisha shifted her attention and energies toward improving her, and her son's, life.

The Envy Block

One of the final blocks to success that we'll discuss before moving on to healing steps is "envy."

Jealousy is often confused with envy, but jealousy is actually a fear of losing something or someone that is valuable to us, while envy means feeling pain while desiring something or somebody. For example, one might feel jealous because a spouse is talking with an attractive member of the opposite sex. The jealousy stems from fears that the spouse likes the new person better. There's a fear of losing the marriage, companionship, and love.

A person might feel envy when looking at someone who seems to have more than he or she does—a better house, car, marriage, body, job, or education. The essential question about envy is: do you use it to inspire or to block you?

— Do you admire a friend's aerobicized figure and vow to get in shape yourself, or do you curse her under your breath and avoid her?

— Do you admire a beautiful mansion, knowing that you too could own such a house if you really wanted to, or do you feel that rich people are evil or crooked?

— Do you admire a neighbor's new car and feel inspired to go car-shopping yourself, or do you judge her to be showing off?

— Do you admire your co-worker completing night school, and ask about enrolling in the college yourself, or do you bitterly think, Well, sure, it's easy for him; he has fewer family responsibilities?

Envy is definitely a double-edged sword that can block or inspire your personal success. When I appeared on *Oprah* recently, discussing weight-loss issues, the television producers shared an interesting pattern with me. After Oprah lost weight using a low-fat diet combined with exercise, many viewers wrote her to comment on how she'd changed.

The letters fell into two main categories: those viewers who detested Oprah's new weight, complaining they could no longer relate to her; and those viewers who admired Oprah's successful weight loss. The producers noticed that every negative letter writer *was also* a person who complained of not being able to lose weight. The letters typically said, "If I had your money, Oprah, I could lose weight, too. I could hire a chef and a personal trainer, but I don't have enough money."

However, without exception, the letter writers who were happy for Oprah's successes were also the people who said she inspired them to lose weight as well.

Studies show that the most successful people are those who are fueled and inspired by other people's victories. Unsuccessful people, on the other hand, are often threatened by others' successes, as if the successful person were stealing some opportunity from the unsuccessful one.

You may want to observe your thoughts and feelings when you are in the company of successful people or when you see a desired object or condition. Notice, without judgment, whether others' achievements inspire your hopes or deflate them. Vow to reprogram any negative reactions towards others' success.

When you see a desired object (house, car, outfit, etc.), tell yourself that you too can own and enjoy that thing. Say something to yourself like, "Isn't it great that we live in a time and place when prosperity is an option for this person, and also for me?" When you view a happily in-love couple, feel pleasure as if they were giving you a gift of vicarious love (which they really are doing!).

View others' successes as inspiration and confirmation that you, too, can have whatever you want. Tell yourself, without a trace of bitterness, that everyone—including yourself, of course—deserves

to have a peaceful, pleasurable life. If there's something about another's life that really excites you, use that feeling to motivate you!
Be thankful that the other person helped you uncover your goals,
so you're now clear about what you want. As we've discussed,
knowing what you want and knowing you deserve it, are two factors that are essential to goal fulfillment.

POINTS TO REMEMBER

🙒 Your sex, upbringing, age, race, creed, or education only
limit you if you believe that they can.

🙒 To grow, prosper, and succeed, it's often necessary to leave
behind familiar situations and habits.

🙒 Jealousy and envy can block you from attaining the type of
lifestyle you want.

🙒　🙒　🙒

A
Schedule
with
Breathing
Room

THERE *REALLY ARE* ENOUGH HOURS
IN THE DAY

*"Dost thou love life? Then do not squander time, for
that is the stuff life is made of."*

— BENJAMIN FRANKLIN

Does it seem like there's a time shortage in your life? Do
you run at a dead heat all day long, yet accomplish very
little? The solution isn't a 26-hour day—it's realistic time
management and prioritizing strategies that put you in control of
your schedule.

Time management is really life management. This means having time for *all* your priorities, including relaxation, family fun,
spiritual growth, exercise, continuing education, and making money.
Phheww! Does the thought of doing all that sound imposing? Well,
there will be some parts of your schedule that may require
streamlining. But don't worry, these are activities you won't miss
at all. We're only going to throw the time-wasting, energy-draining activities over the side of your hot air balloon so you can feel
lighter and go higher.

Step One: Your Priorities

Desire fulfillment begins with getting your time under control.
Happy and successful people use their time well, while dissatisfied

people waste their time on empty activities. Low-priority endeavors drain self-esteem, energy, and enthusiasm.

The first step in taking control of your time is to acknowledge and write down a list of your priorities. The only way to know whether you're wasting your time is to be aware of what is important to you. Priorities are different from goals. Priorities are umbrella categories such as "God and spirituality," "personal health," "children," or "money." Goals are detailed, specific items that fall under the priority umbrella. For example, a goal underneath the "health" priority might be, "Exercise for 30 minutes, 3 times a week."

Many people have two priority lists:

1. Their "true" priority list, and
2. A "should" priority list.

These individuals may be afraid to admit to themselves or others what they truly want. So, they work on what they believe "should" be their priority. For example, my client Becky's true priority was "children." She really wanted to start a family and stay home with her kids. Yet, she felt this priority was "incorrect," and that she "should" instead value her career and making money.

When we hold both true and false priority lists, the natural results are stress and confusion. It's like having one foot on the gas pedal and one on the brakes while trying to drive your car. How could Becky best know how to prioritize her schedule? After all, a priority of "children" requires different actions than a priority of "career."

A few of my clients discovered that they had two priority lists because they wanted to please their parents. For example, on his "should" list, Tony's top priority was completing his law degree (his parents' top priority for him) and on his "true" list, Tony's top priority was buying a house in the country. When he came to see me for counseling, Tony was understandably confused.

What's most important is to follow your gut feelings when deciding where your true priorities lie. If you are indecisive, mentally "try on" different scenarios and see which one brings you the greatest peace of mind. When you follow your natural inclinations toward peace and progress, you can be certain that these are God-given instructions that form your Divine Purpose. Trust that He would not give you an assignment without backing it up with sufficient time, money, and talent to fulfill the entire plan.

Here is a place to write your top five *true* priorities. You'll want to review and possibly update this list every few months. Keep this list in mind, and you'll be clear about how to spend the spare time you create.

MY TRUE PRIORITIES

1._____

2._____

3._____

4._____

5._____

Step Two: Your Time Inventory

The next step with respect to getting control of your time is to conduct a "Time Inventory" to assess where your time is currently being spent. To do this, keep a small notebook with you, and write an hour-by-hour diary of your activities for one full week. For example:

SATURDAY

11:00—Cleaned house
12:00—Grocery shopping
1:00—Talked with Sue
2:00—Wrote a letter to Mom
3:00—Watched television

I first did this exercise in an undergraduate psychology class on "Death and Dying." The time inventory taught me that I had a finite number of years on earth, and if I were going to accomplish my goals, I'd best get started now. I urge you to try this exercise, and you'll find that it really ignites your motivation.

By the way, you can ask your intuition to tell you what age you'll live to. When I ask my gut, "How old will I live to be?," I get the answer, "82." Everyone I share this information with is also able to get a number from their intuition. It's very motivating to know how long you'll live, because you know how many years you have in order to fulfill your divine assignment.

After you complete and review your time inventory, you'll likely notice many time-wasting activities that run counter to your goals or desires. Decide to modify any ineffective parts of your schedule today! This doesn't mean becoming a workaholic, since family and relaxation time are probably among your highest priorities. It means stopping time-bleeding activities, like reading the entire newspaper, purposeless telephone conversations, or watching television shows that you don't care about.

Step Three: A Firm Commitment

Now that you're clear about your priorities and schedule, it's time to seal the deal with yourself. The difference between a goal and a wish is commitment:

You *plan* to accomplish a goal.
You *hope* you'll get a wish.

See the difference? No wonder goals create results, while wishes merely chew away our lives.

Nothing gets accomplished until you *plan* to manifest something. In Part One of the book, we confronted blocks that could make you doubt your abilities or deservingness. We dealt with procrastination habits, and you read about the importance of giving yourself permission to make life changes and achieve your goals.

Now, nothing stands in your way, so let's turn your divine assignment and its accompanying goals and priorities into reality. You really are going to make this happen!

I've found that many people are better at keeping promises to other people than they are at keeping the promises they make to themselves. That's one reason why people say, "I'll start my diet next Monday," and then Monday rolls around and they reschedule the goal for the following week. This is a natural human tendency, and instead of fighting it, we're going to capitalize upon it for your personal benefit.

On the following page, there is a "Firm Commitment" form for you to photocopy. Complete, sign, and date this form, and then hang it in a conspicuous location such as on a bathroom mirror, car dashboard, personal bulletin board, or refrigerator door—somewhere where you'll see it once or twice a day. If you're concerned about other people seeing this form, put it in a private place that you will definitely see every day, such as your purse, wallet, briefcase, or bathroom drawer.

MY FIRM COMMITMENT STATEMENT

I,_____ , definitely want
to change my life for the better right now. I declare that the following priorities are important to me, and that I now choose
to take charge of my time for the fulfillment of these priorities:

1._____

2._____

3._____

4._____

5._____

I know that my mental, physical, spiritual, financial, and
family health is dependent upon my being happy and enthused
about my life. I also know that I will be more joyful and inspired by spending consistent time toward the fulfillment of my
priorities. I also know that I have a purpose to accomplish, and
that my priorities form a basis for fulfilling this purpose. I trust
that by making this firm commitment, I will have enough time,
money, talent, and support for the accomplishment of my desires. All I have to do is trust and heed my priorities.

Signature:_____

Date: _____

What Is Important to You?

Most people are busy, but few feel content and successful. If we're going to expend effort anyway, it makes sense to channel our energies in ways that yield satisfaction for ourselves and our family. A subtle shift to adopting these four success habits can make the difference between hectic misery and enthusiastic happiness.

FOUR QUALITIES OF HAPPY, SUCCESSFUL PEOPLE

1. *A focus on results.* Happy and successful people measure their effective use of time by the *results* of their efforts. Dissatisfied people only point to how busy and hard they've worked, or create excuses why they didn't accomplish more.

2. *Knowing the value of their time.* Happy and successful people continually ask themselves, "What's the most valuable use of my time right now?" They never do anything of a second-order priority when a higher-order priority is left undone. These winners also know how to identify and eliminate time-wasters, such as needless meetings, drop-in visitors, reading the entire newspaper, going grocery shopping every day, over-commitment, procrastination, and crisis management. If someone asks that they do something that doesn't contribute to the accomplishment of their most important goals, they have the strength and character to say, "No!"

3. *Knowing their priorities.* Successful, happy people know their priorities. Each day, they ask themselves, "What do I need to accomplish today to bring me closer to achieving my priorities?" They don't waste time at work with office politics or gossip because they're concentrating on completing their priorities. They understand the importance of focusing on projects that yield the highest emotional, spiritual, and financial gains.

4. *Efficiency.* An intense focus during the work day always brings positive results. First, these happy, successful people complete their priorities and receive emotional, financial, and career rewards. Second, they leave work with clear consciences, knowing they've finished a productive day's work. Their energy is high and their schedules more free, so they have time to exercise, relax, and enjoy their family. They know the truth of this revelation: *You don't need to do more to achieve success; you just need to spend more time working on activities you value rather than on those that are insignificant.*

Sticking to Your Priorities

You'll find yourself elated by every step you take toward the accomplishment of your goals. On the other hand, you'll feel tired, frustrated, and dragged down every day in which you don't accomplish something important to you.

It's tragically ironic that those projects most valuable to us seem the most difficult to start. Yet, once we complete an important project, we feel more exhilarated than if we'd worked on a million inconsequential tasks!

The simple act of writing down your goals, as we did in Chapter 3, will make you feel more energized and give you higher self-esteem than just about anything else you could do. You'll feel even more terrific if you devote 10 minutes every day toward achieving those goals. Conversely, if you work toward something that is unexciting to you, you'll end up feeling tired, bored, or even depressed.

To stick with your priorities, review them every morning and ask yourself, "What can I do today that will bring me closer to achieving my goals?" Every moment, you are either working on something of value (and again, that includes any goals of relaxation or free time), or you are engaged in something insignificant.

One of the most important habits you can establish that will guarantee your success is to *reread your priorities daily!* Each morning, instead of wasting time reading the back of cereal boxes, eating a large breakfast, or watching television, ask yourself, "What can I do today that will help me achieve my top priority?" Then, write down the exact steps you are going to accomplish during that day. Make a list, so you can cross off your accomplishments as they are completed.

> Dava Gerard, M.D., a noted female physician whose priority is curing breast cancer, credits her career and personal success to her daily habit of organized goal-setting. "When I think of a goal, I write it down on paper," she explains, "and that way I don't have the thought spinning around in my head anymore."
>
> Every morning, Dr. Gerard writes down her goals for the day. "Those who review their long-term goals daily are always rewarded," she advises. "Be sure to set priorities, and don't just do the easy stuff on your goal list. Push yourself to do the hard work that it takes to get what you want."

Make yourself work on your most important priorities before engaging in less meaningful tasks. If this means getting up earlier, then do so. Many people avoid or procrastinate working on their most personally meaningful goals. They are afraid—afraid of failure, afraid of success, afraid of ridicule. However, those major projects won't get completed on their own. When we don't work on them, our inner guide nags at us and puts pressure on us to get going. The voice of the inner guide—which knows our true function and purpose for living—won't stop nagging until we get to work on our priorities. The happiest, most successful people understand this concept, and develop the habit of working on first things first.

Organized goal-setting, using written long- and short-term strategies as we've outlined here, automatically knocks down a great deal of fear. It's so much easier to face small increments that eventually add up to a big accomplishment than to feel over-whelmed by a seemingly enormous goal.

Every day, take one step toward your goal, and your dreams will rapidly come true.

Most people find that their written goals become realities much faster than they expect. Just the act of writing down a goal gives you the focus and energy to make that goal come about at turbo-speed.

A Realtor named Karen, whom I know socially, smashed sales records during the country's worst housing market. Karen says her practice of writing down long- and short-term goals instantly cre-ated results for her. "Last year," she told me, "I accomplished my two-year income goal: to make a quarter million in commissions within three months."

You don't need to do more than you're already doing to create the life of your dreams. You only need to distinguish *valuable ac-tivities*—those actions that bring you closer to your goals—from *insignificant activities*—those actions that take you away from your goals. The super-successful and happy person spends most of the time on valuable activities, and very little (or no) time on in-significant activities. He or she continually asks before acting, "Is this activity bringing me closer to, or farther away from, my goals?"

Vicki Lansky, the bestselling baby-food cookbook author we met in Chapter 6, keeps a sign on her desk that keeps her focused on her priorities: *"What I do today is important, because I'm ex-changing one day of my life for it."*

The Time Crunch and Stress

The main source of stress on the job is feeling a lack of control over your time. As mentioned earlier, research shows that secre-taries, for example, have more stress than their bosses because they are not in control of, nor can they always predict, their work agen-das. A 1990 Cornell University study concluded that jobs com-bining high responsibility with low autonomy were three times more likely to produce high blood pressure than jobs that either offered some degree of autonomy or lower responsibility levels.

Symptoms of stress, such as back or neck pain, compulsive behavior, absenteeism, defensiveness, fatigue, and insomnia, are signs that something is wrong. Instead of ignoring these signs, successful and happy people take action, which might involve looking for a new job or making changes at their present job to lower their stress level. If you can work on an activity that holds more meaning for you, you automatically reduce negative effects of work stress.

We all know the importance of exercise and proper sleep and nutrition in helping us deal with stress. Yet, dissatisfied people who feel stressed often fail to exercise regularly, or they overeat or overdrink. Happy, successful people, constantly aware of their priorities and schedules, take care of their bodies. They view exercise and healthful habits as a necessity, not an optional luxury, and they don't make excuses or feel guilty about taking the time to work out their bodies. This commitment to a healthful lifestyle yields a positive outlook, as well as the energy that is necessary in order to deal with life's challenges.

Beyond Fast-Track Mentality

In the '80s, many of us went on buying binges. We accumulated cars, appliances, and other excesses—often paid for on credit. Getting caught up in the frenzy of materialism was so easy, fueled by adrenaline and competitiveness. Most of us believed we'd find some sort of happiness once we drove our expensive import cars to the end of the rainbow.

Today, we've seen how hollow all that fast-track stuff was. Now, we want more time for meaningful endeavors. We are no longer willing to sacrifice time with our children or spouse. Still, many people feel squeezed by too-tight budgets and too-tight schedules. Although we've adopted more family values, the mortgage and electricity bills still scream, "Pay me!" We're also painfully aware of the need for consistent exercise, and we search diligently for that extra one hour a day for a yoga class or a set of tennis.

Money can't buy happiness, but the fact remains that upper-income people have the lowest divorce and suicide rates in America. The biggest lie ever told is that rich people are miserable! After all, wealth buys time to spend with your family, the freedom to change careers, better health care, education for yourself and your children, comfortable cars, and homes in safe neighborhoods.

There's a big difference, however, between accumulating material goods on credit, and having financial security and independence. There really is an alternative to the excess of the '80s and the too-tight schedules/too-tight budgets of the '90s!

Fortunately, research shows that you don't have to sacrifice success to enjoy a fulfilling home and family life. The most successful and happy people I know use their 9-to-5 moments following their intuition's direction in some career venture. These folks have abundant money and happiness because they have surrendered to their intuition's guidance. They put in a full day's work toward fulfilling their divine assignment, and so their priorities receive adequate attention.

Unhappy people, in contrast, feel overwhelmed and underpaid because they don't control their schedules. Needless socializing, meetings, and telephone calls waste a staggering number of hours each day. No wonder their priorities are unattended, and the person screams, "There aren't enough hours in the day!" The pressure of unfinished dreams drains both energy and confidence.

The happiest people I have met don't waste one minute of time at work. So, instead of arriving home worried and discouraged about unfinished work, they feel energized by their day's accomplishments. Super women and men? No, simply superorganized and focused women and men. That's what "working smart" means, after all. Like stretching a dollar to stay within a budget, people who work smart, productively use each minute (without becoming workaholics).

If we don't complete our work while we're at the office, one of three consequences usually occurs:

1. The work is completed during hours that could be spent in more meaningful ways, such as relaxing with the family, exercising, taking a night course, or meditating.
2. The career stagnates; or layoffs, demotions, or firings occur.
3. Low wages and mismatched careers create personal dissatisfaction.

None of these options are particularly desirable, are they? Fortunately, when we focus and prioritize in the workplace, these three options are avoidable in the first place. You needn't sacrifice family and personal fulfillment on your way to success. In fact, lasting success isn't possible unless you have first achieved harmony within yourself.

Don't Look Down!

Once you've pinpointed what you want, and you've decided that nothing will stand in your way, you'll experience a dramatic rise in confidence and enthusiasm. Doors of opportunity will open, and amazing coincidences will happen as if by magic.

As you begin your momentum forward, it's important to keep going. Don't let your new forward motion frighten you in any way. Reread Part 1 of this book if you ever find yourself thinking, "Oh no! My goal is coming true and it scares me!"

As you climb up, don't ever look down, or you may lose your balance.

POINTS TO REMEMBER

❧ The happiest, most successful people all take control of their schedules and make time for relaxation, exercise, and relationships.

❧ Three steps for taking control of your time include making a Priority List, taking a Time Inventory, and making a Firm Commitment toward the fulfillment of your goals.

❧ Job stress comes from having an out-of-control schedule.

❧ To achieve more of your goals, spend more time on valuable activities and less time on insignificant ones.

❧ It's important to focus and concentrate on accomplishing desired results during work hours so you can enjoy your after-work hours.

❧ Don't let your new heights of success frighten you.

❧ ❧ ❧

THE TOP TEN TIME WASTERS

"I would if I could, stand on a busy corner, hat in hand and beg people to throw me all their wasted hours."
— BERNARD BERENSON (1865–1959),
AMERICAN HISTORIAN

You've probably heard the old maxim, "Expenses always rise to the level of your income." For example, a person gets a $5,000 raise and then immediately buys a new, more expensive car.

Well, our schedules aren't much different. When you detailed your exact dreams and goals, you essentially gave yourself a "time raise." You'll now have a little more breathing room in your schedule. The question is, will your "time expenses" now rise to the level of your new schedule? In other words, will you allow new time-wasters to rob you of the time you've committed toward the accomplishment of your goals?

Like squandering hundreds of dollars on unnecessary purchases, it's so easy to waste countless hours unknowingly that you could instead invest in meaningful activities.

Don't rob yourself of precious opportunities that can make the difference between health and illness, between family harmony and discord, or between financial security and stressful insecurity. Remember: it's your time. You choose how you want to use it!

Time Robbers

I had a dramatic experience that reminded me how much I am in charge of my life. For several months, I had been frustrated because I was getting between 20 and 50 calls a day from people who wanted my help. Now, I didn't mind—and still don't mind—the calls I received from people wanting to become counseling clients. What was bothering me were the calls from people wanting free advice about how to make more money. These were quasi-colleagues, not friends, who were asking for guidance on ways to boost their incomes.

Of course, as a committed helping professional, I would offer a bit of advice to each of these callers. But several of these individuals began taking habitual advantage of my generosity. They would call me a couple of times a week just to complain about how broke they were. They'd describe various schemes for making money, and then list the reasons why they wouldn't work. These men and women seemingly weren't interested in doing anything concrete to improve their situations; they just wanted a sympathetic ear.

I felt victimized. I was unsure of how to handle the situation, and felt stuck between my priority of helping people and that of taking care of my own needs and those of my family. Yet, there I was, giving away dozens of hours a week to people who didn't even seem to care about my income or my schedule. At the end of each phone call, *they'd* feel better, but *I'd* feel drained and angry. I was irritable, but conflicted, about how to put an end to this time-robbing cycle.

It took a dramatic incident to help me solve my dilemma.

Warned and Protected

We always attract situations and people into our lives that perfectly match our overriding beliefs, and I certainly attracted a doozy! One Saturday afternoon during this trying and confusing time, I was getting ready to go to a seminar about intuition. As I was showering, a voice (which I believe to be a guardian angel) told me, "Doreen, you'd better put the top up on your car, or it will get stolen." I was in a hurry, though, and putting up the convertible top would require an extra five minutes. So I chose to ignore the voice. Still, it continued its warnings to beware of car thieves.

I figured that my car might be stolen while I was in the seminar, but for some reason I trusted that everything would work out okay. My car was paid-in-full and I only carried liability, so insurance wouldn't reimburse it if someone stole it. Still, I knew without a doubt that God would protect the car and me.

While driving to the school, I listened to a cassette tape of *A Course in Miracles* that explained how we all have spiritual helpers alongside us. As I pulled into the parking lot, an eerie feeling surrounded me, as if someone had spotted my car and intended to steal it. I decided to spread some spiritual books across the dashboard of the car, prayed for protection, and visualized the vehicle surrounded by the white light of God.

I no sooner stood up to get out of my car than a man rushed up to me, grabbed my purse handle, and demanded my car keys. I looked into the man's eyes and saw an expression of pure fear. I, on the other hand, felt strong and backed up by spiritual protection. I had a choice to hand over my car keys and purse, or to say "No!"

I chose the latter and screamed with every ounce of air in my lungs. The man looked at me with shock, and his focus shifted from stealing my car to stealing my purse. The more frightened he looked, though, the more powerful I felt. I was determined that he would not steal *anything* that belonged to me!

Finally, my screaming attracted people from the school, and their presence made the man stop pulling on my purse handle, and he ran away. When I called the police later, I learned that the car-jacker had a gun and a knife. God had warned and protected me, without a doubt!

The Lesson

After the attempted car-jacking, I spent two weeks assessing my life. Knowing we are responsible for everything that happens to us, I needed to figure out why I attracted this crime into my life.

Finally, I realized the reason: it showed me how much choice over my life circumstances I have. I had a choice during the car-jacking whether or not to hand over my purse and car keys. My firm commitment not to be robbed changed the balance of the situation. The thief was afraid. I, on the other hand, was determined. My positive intent and energy overpowered his negativity and fear.

I had clearly been *allowing* people to rob me of my time, just as the car thief wanted me to allow him to take my car. Instead of being angry with the callers for robbing my time, I needed to take proactive action and just quit saying "yes." Amazingly, after I told the callers that I was busy, they disappeared as quickly as they had originally appeared in my life. The sky didn't fall on my head, and nothing bad happened. I learned, in dramatic fashion, an important lesson about time and life ownership.

My inner guide had warned me that I was allowing telephone calls to interfere with fulfilling my priorities. It also warned me that my car was going to be stolen. The inner guide is never wrong, but our ego—which fights and resists the inner guide's wisdom—is always wrong. The ego can be only be counted upon to do one thing: deliver destructive information. My car-jacking taught me how crucial it is to follow my intuition, for the very sake of my life. Today, while I must admit that I don't *always* trust my intuition, I nevertheless *always* follow it without question or hesitation. Blind faith in intuition always pays enormous dividends.

Identifying Time and Energy Wasters

As I did, you probably have multiple priorities including family, health, and finances. Given all those concerns, you don't need time robbers in your life, do you? Here are the top ten time and energy wasters to watch out for. In the three chapters that follow, we'll discuss practical ways for taking control of your schedule.

TOP TEN TIME AND ENERGY WASTERS

1. Procrastination pals
2. Sport fighting
3. Not prioritizing
4. Meaningless meetings
5. Disorganization
6. Overeating
7. Mindless media
8. Saying "yes" when you'd rather say "no"
9. Not delegating
10. Indecision and worry

1. *Procrastination pals:* These are "friends" who are afraid of committing to their own goals, so they covertly agree to procrastinate with you. Procrastination pals call or stop by your home or office to complain about their awful work or love lives. If anyone suggests that they could improve their lives, procrastination pals recite negative clichés, such as "Dream on," "I wish," "Get real," or "If something can go wrong, it will." Procrastination pals require extremely high maintenance, causing you to waste many valuable hours of your time.

   We enter procrastination "paldom" for unhealthy reasons, such as a need to be needed, a fear of offending, or the desire to rescue people (which is really a projection of wishing someone would rescue us!). Usually, we hope that if we give the procrastination pal enough time, advice, and love, he or she will come around and become an independent and happy person. We may even hope for rewards for the role we played in the rescue operation.

These are futile hopes, though, because procrastination pals are chronically in love with their high-drama problems. Many are even addicted to the adrenaline rush of a roller-coaster lifestyle. You don't need to stick around to see how their movie-of-the-week turns out, and you don't need their permission to opt out of this unhealthy relationship. Put your time and energy to better use, in ways that really will heal the world.

Sometimes, though, we use procrastination pals to validate our fears about making progress toward our dreams. If you surround yourself with enough people who share the view that "nice guys finish last," or "I'll always struggle financially," it feels safer to not even try. No matter what the basis for the procrastination pal relationship, you can probably see why it's the main time and energy waster.

2. *Sport fighting.* Conflict drains your energy, happiness, and time! Fortunately, fighting doesn't have to be a part of your life. Although roommates, spouses, and co-workers are bound to disagree occasionally, some people *create* needless arguments out of insecurity or boredom. I call this "sport fighting." Versions of sport fighting include:

    — "Let's you and he fight," where co-workers invent problems to entertain themselves at work.
    — "We haven't fought in a week; what's wrong?," where couples get in a habit of arguing just for the sake of arguing.
    — "If it wasn't for you, I would accomplish my goals," where a blame game masks procrastination and fears.

You can save yourself much time and grief by pausing a moment, instead of automatically sport fighting. Ask yourself, "Is this really important to me? What other options do I have instead of arguing?" Some alternatives to fighting are: writing down your feelings in a journal; walking away from the argument; going outside or taking a walk; suggesting to the other person that you two calmly discuss the issue; making a future appointment where you two can negotiate a solution; and seeking counseling.

3. *Not prioritizing.* If you don't clearly know what your first, second, third, fourth, and fifth priorities are, you will always feel you've forgotten to do something. This little nagging feeling is your gut instinct urging you to fulfill your priorities. Take 30 minutes and list your 5 top priorities, and you'll never again spin your wheels with indecision about how to spend your time.

4. *Meaningless meetings.* How many hours a week do you spend in meetings, painfully writhing in your seat with boredom and time pressures? You probably can skip meetings or leave them early if you explain your more pressing needs (which increase the company's bottom line) to your boss. You will impress your supervisor with your industriousness, and you will be relieved of time-wasting meetings!

   Meaningless meetings also include those seminars that promise the moon but deliver run-of-the-mill information you could have gotten by reading a book. Before signing up for the next wonderful-sounding seminar, call ahead of time and ask for an outline of exactly what topics will be covered. Better yet, skip the seminar and just read the facilitator's book. You'll save hundreds of dollars and probably get more thorough answers to your questions.

5. *Disorganization.* Depending upon one's organizational habits, you can either save or you can lose three to five hours a day. Disorganized closets, drawers, and desks cost needless time, anxiety, and even money while hunting for an important item. Disorganized shopping trips are another time-waster. Stream-

line your shopping into a planned excursion, avoid busy shopping days and times (weekends, holidays, or 5:00 P.M. on weekdays) or daily grocery shopping. Call ahead to see if the store stocks your desired item. I highly recommend investing time in organizing your home and office so you'll know where everything is. It's also visually refreshing to see a neat area. I'd also like you to consider "Feng Shui" as a way of organizing the places where you live and work. Feng Shui, the ancient Chinese art of placement, says that each area of a structure (or individual room) corresponds to an emotional or physical area of our lives—such as the Health and Family area, the Prosperity corner, or the Romance and Marriage corner. You can find out more about Feng Shui in the wonderful book, *The Western Guide to Feng Shui,* by Terah Kathryn Collins (Hay House, 1996).

6. *Overeating.* Another waste of time is eating two or three helpings of a meal. It gives the illusion of doing something important—after all, we have to eat!—yet it accomplishes nothing. I've worked with many clients who felt frustrated because they would regularly binge-eat at breakfast time. I find that this behavior is a way of procrastinating facing the day and getting started. Instead of doing chores, it's easier to curl up in front of a bottomless bowl of breakfast cereal.

7. *Mindless media.* It's pleasurable to watch a wonderful television program or a movie, or to read a great book or magazine. Yet there's a big difference between *purposeful* media entertainment—a program or book you've been looking forward to—and *mindless* media entertainment where you watch anything that's on television out of boredom. The way to tell the difference is to see if you can recall the contents of the program or reading material the next day. With mindless media, you won't remember a thing. This includes news-

paper reading—reading the entire paper from front to back takes hours. Why not, instead, skim the headlines and ask yourself whether you are interested in the story? You'll save time and skip a lot of negativity.

8. *Saying "yes" when you'd rather say "no."* Your neighbor stops by for coffee and a long chat. Your son wants you to drive him across town to his friend's house. Your co-workers want you to join them Friday night. These activities are fine if you genuinely want to say "yes."

Often, we say "yes" because of fears or a false sense of obligation. Not only is our time wasted, but we feel resentment during the undesirable activity. Of course, resentment chews away energy and self-esteem. If your gut tells you to say "no," then say it. Trust that obeying this instinct serves everybody's best interests, since your gut feelings guide you toward peace of mind and fulfillment.

Often, people lace their undesirable requests with flattery or guilt-producing statements such as, "You're the only one who can do it," or "Without you, we'd never get anything done." However, they'll find another "one and only" person very quickly if you turn down their request. Remember, you'll feel a greater sense of accomplishment and self-worth by spending that time on your priorities and goals.

9. *Not delegating.* Many of my clients complain that housework overwhelms them. Invariably, I find that they are not asking or insisting that children or spouses help. Any child over the age of four benefits from doing chores. It makes them feel important and helps the parents. I recommend having regular family meetings, where you discuss and assign chores—and that includes your spouse! If your family members aren't doing a quality job, be sure and discuss this with them. Some women feel that their self-worth depends upon being a

Superwoman at home; I hope you won't indulge in such a delusion.

Delegating is also important outside the home. Don't feel you have to do everything at the office or the store. Ask for help, even if it feels uncomfortable. The cooperation you'll get from others will amaze you! Soon, asking for help becomes a comfortably positive habit that frees up extra hours and energy.

10. *Indecision and worry.* Should I leave Tom, or try to work out the relationship with him? Should I quit my job and return to college? What if my company lays me off and I can't find another job right away? Indecision and worry are negative mental habits that serve no useful purpose. Ruminating this way and that way about all the possible options in your work, love, or family life wastes time and gets you nowhere closer to your goals.

To decide quickly and easily, imagine your different options as if mentally trying each one on. See which options yield the most peace of mind, and choose that one. Stick to that choice, and do not allow yourself to think "what if" thoughts about the other options.

You can stop worrying in the same way. Write down everything that troubles you, and vow to take constructive action where you can, and let go of situations you cannot control (such as other people's actions or feelings). Lean on your spiritual trust, remembering that God has never allowed you to starve in the past, and He will always take care of you in the future.

POINTS TO REMEMBER

- You have the right to say "no" to time-robbing people and situations.

- The top time waster, procrastination pals, are those people who we covertly agree to join with, validating one another's excuses for delaying success.

- Negative emotional habits also waste our valuable time and energy. These include disorganization, not knowing our priorities, worrying, and being indecisive.

CHAPTER NINE

SETTING YOUR TIME LIMITS

*"Let us make up our minds that yesterday is gone.
Tomorrow has not yet arrived. But today can be filled
with wonder if we know that we stand on the threshold
of that which is wonderful and new."*

— ERNEST HOLMES, AUTHOR OF
THE SCIENCE OF MIND

No matter what you want—more free time, more money, or more education, you can have it. Decide that you will no longer delay living the life that you want. Take action now! Every goal consists of many little steps, in the same way that pennies and dollars compose a big bank account. Investing even *ten minutes* a day toward the life that you want will yield *huge* benefits:

+ *Increased life satisfaction.* Just knowing that you are headed in your desired direction elevates your mood.
+ *Increased energy.* You'll feel excited by the steps you are taking, and your enthusiasm boosts your energy.
+ *Increased productivity.* Your higher energy level carries over into other areas of your life, inspiring you to whistle while you work.
+ *Increased opportunities.* When you focus on your goal, you'll automatically notice and capitalize upon books, classes,

institutions, and professionals who could help you achieve
your objectives.

✦ *Increased "co-incidences."* As if by a mysterious force, people,
circumstances, money, and information will appear in your life
to guide you to the next level of accomplishment.

Three Ways to Accomplish Anything

There is no "secret" to success, except having a strong desire to
create the life about which you dream, and the determination to follow through. You can have anything you want, unless you believe
otherwise. It doesn't matter what your life is currently like. No matter how time-consuming your job is, how many family obligations
you have, what your financial status is, the amount of education or
training you have, or what condition your body is in, if you want
something badly enough, you *will* achieve it! Think about any success you've ever achieved, and you'll remember that behind it all
was your determination. If you've succeeded once, you can succeed
again.

Here are three important steps you can take right now to move
toward the accomplishment of your desires:

1. *Break down the goal into little steps.* You've probably heard
   statements such as "write one page a day, and in a year you've
   completed a book." Well, it is true, and we accomplish most
   goals in the same one-step-a-day manner. Recall any of your
   major accomplishments, and you'll see how they consisted of
   many little steps. All other goals are identical, without exception!

2. *Perform one step a day.* Academy Award nominee Sally Kirk-
   land, during a lecture at my school, said that she did one thing
   every day to enhance her career. It could be any one thing: a
   phone call to a casting director, mailing a résumé to a producer,

or reading a script. What she did wasn't as important as the momentum she produced in her career by putting forth small daily efforts.

I agree with the concept of consistent daily efforts. If you approach your goal on an inconsistent, random basis, you're apt to lose interest in the project. However, if you devote just ten minutes a day to it, you'll soon develop an automatic positive habit. Don't worry about what steps you need to take tomorrow. *You will know what to do when tomorrow comes.* Just perform the steps required today, and let the dream naturally emerge into a reality.

3. *Write down a schedule for these steps in ink on your calendar.* It's a good idea to set a realistic timetable for your daily goal-fulfilling sessions. When I wrote my first book, I inked a writing schedule on my calendar. It was the only way I could be sure I'd accomplish anything! After all, I had a full-time job, two small children, a husband, night-school classes, and an exercise schedule. I *really* wanted to write that book, so I made a schedule and stuck to it.

I wrote my first book from 9 to 10:00 P.M. every night, when the kids were asleep. I found extra time here and there to write by turning down social events, such as going to the movies or restaurants. Yes, I would have rather been at parties than at home writing, but I was determined to fulfill my dream. The day my book arrived from the publisher, I knew my social "sacrifices" were worth it. The heartfelt thank-you letters I received from readers further confirmed my sentiments.

POINTS TO REMEMBER

🙠 Simply making the decision to achieve your goal will increase your energy and self-esteem.

🙠 Any person can accomplish any goal in small time chunks consistently applied on a daily basis.

🙠 Don't worry about *how* you will attain your goal; just focus on performing one step today toward its accomplishment.

🙠 Break the goal down into little steps, do one step a day, and write down a realistic schedule for its achievement.

*More
Time
for
You!*

YOU *DO* HAVE TIME TO EXERCISE

"I wasted time, and now doth time waste me."
— FROM *RICHARD II*, BY WILLIAM SHAKESPEARE

A ll goals are essentially the same, because they all boil down to the same basic process:

+ Deciding what you want;
+ Creating passion, faith, and determination about your desire;
+ Setting a realistic schedule of small steps, and—most importantly—
+ Keeping your promises to yourself.

In the first few pages of *A Course in Miracles*, we are introduced to an essential concept: *There is no order of difficulty in miracles.* One miracle is as difficult or as easy to manifest as any other. It's only our human egos that decide that one is harder than another! But our higher self knows that miracles are natural, and so is success.

As I discussed earlier, most goals center around one of three life areas: health, love, and money. We looked at how these life areas form tips of a triangle. In the next three chapters, we'll look at specific ways to enjoy satisfaction in each area. Here are suggestions—some earthly, some not—about how to have more time to devote to your priorities.

The first life area we'll look at is "health," specifically, exercise. Exercise is extremely important to your health and well-being, as you probably know. In fact, some exercise equipment now carries the U.S. Surgeon General's warning: *"The Surgeon General has determined that lack of physical exercise is detrimental to your health."* Really!

Over 64 percent of Americans say they don't have time to exercise, according to a survey by the President's Council on Physical Fitness. Yet, the same survey revealed that 84 percent of Americans watch television at least three hours a week! Clearly, extra time isn't the problem here. It's a lack of motivation and time-management practices.

Let's see if we can tackle the problem right here, right now.

Exercise Procrastination

It's too hot. You're too tired. The kids have the sniffles. The gym's too crowded. When we're faced with the choice of whether or not to exercise, the world readily provides us with a million reasons for staying sedentary. Take Terry, for example:

> Terry, a 38-year-old mother of two who attended one of my workshops, said she couldn't fit exercise into her schedule. She was forever slamming into the wall of family and work responsibilities and couldn't find a spare five minutes for relaxation, let alone a couple of hours to go to the gym.
>
> She had purchased several gym memberships in the past, and every time, her gym card sat unused in her wallet until it finally expired. Terry decided to try exercising at home, so she bought a workout tape. Well, that plan lasted three days before Terry became bored with the whole thing.

I asked Terry to name her main objections to exercise. She didn't hesitate, as she responded, "Boredom, boredom, boredom."

Many people that I speak to feel guilty or stressed because they know they "should" exercise regularly, but they just don't want to. Exercise can be strenuous and monotonous, to be sure. And when you're up to your eyeballs in daily responsibilities, it's even more difficult to strap on those gym shoes. Fortunately, being a busy working mother myself, I have developed realistic strategies for fitting exercise into a hectic lifestyle.

It's Worth It!

The benefits of regular exercise far outweigh its costs as to the time, trouble, and sweat invested. One major benefit for busy people is that, after exercise, you feel so energized. That extra boost of energy certainly gives *me* a couple of extra productive hours every day. So it's really a way of doubling your "time investment." Exercise for one hour, and you get additional energy for two more hours in return. I would probably be dragging around the house, groggy and lethargic, if I didn't exercise. However, after a workout, my new vigor means that I get things done in half the time.

In fact, energy is the chief reason I exercise. The fact that it slims my figure, is healthful, and keeps my appetite in check are lesser, secondary benefits. I work out for one reason only: to have more "up" time during each day. Without exercise, I probably couldn't maintain my busy home and work life.

Your Exercise Personality

People who exercise regularly love the benefits of working out. But even fitness buffs have moments when lacing up those sneakers takes more effort than an S.A.T. exam. What's the problem? Often, it stems from boredom. Terry, like many other people I've talked with, said she didn't exercise because of this very issue. Almost always, these feelings arise because people are choosing a workout plan that doesn't mesh with their personality and lifestyle.

I have identified 11 Exercise Personality Characteristics that need to be considered when choosing a fitness program. If you have consistently become bored with exercise, don't blame yourself for being lazy or unmotivated. Most likely, you've just chosen a fitness plan that doesn't suit you. Here are some personality characteristics that you might relate to, which will help you pinpoint the workout plan that will coincide with your particular lifestyle.

EXERCISE PERSONALITY CHARACTERISTICS

1. *A need for intellectual stimulation.* Do monotonous exercise routines drive you batty with boredom? If you have a high need for intellectual stimulation, there are several easy ways to overcome the exercise doldrums. You'll be more motivated to exercise if you read while using a stationary bicycle or stair climber, or listen to the radio or watch television while running on a treadmill. Alternatively, seek out engrossing activities requiring intense concentration and skill, such as yoga or rock climbing.

2. *Creative expressiveness.* Are you an artist at heart? If you have a strong need for creative expression, you would most likely enjoy activities such as ballet, figure skating, or modern dance.

3. *An interest in the mind/body connection.* Are you exercising for stress management, to lose weight, to improve muscle tone, or all of the above? If you answered the latter, a total mind-body-spirit fitness program—such as tai chi—is in

order. If, however, you're after a purely physical activity, then a ski machine or weight lifting would suit your personality. Those who desire both a physical and emotional high would enjoy in-line skating, mountain biking, or tennis.

4. *Challenge.* Some people thrive on challenge, while others prefer to have their exercise go down easy. If you like fast-paced, think-on-your-feet activities, then you'll do well with racquetball or downhill skiing. If you're not crazy about challenges, then you'll likely find methodical, rhythmic workouts such as power walking or stairclimbing more enjoyable.

5. *Peace versus power.* If you enjoy a big dose of thrills and chills to spice up your life, you'll love sports such as kayaking, rock climbing, or snowboarding. If your predilection leans more toward peaceful activities, you'd be better off heading to the pool for some soothing and safe water workouts.

6. *Going solo or side-by-side.* How do you feel about having company when you exercise? Some people prefer to work out alone, while others need a companion for motivation. Some people prefer a close-knit group activity such as volleyball or softball. Still others do well in a large, anonymous crowd such as an aerobics class. If you're a solo player, you'll likely enjoy bicycling or swimming, while others will enjoy these activities with the company of a spouse or a close friend.

7. *Playfulness potential.* Are you a little kid at heart? Someone who loves to climb on the park swings when nobody is looking? Then you need a dose of play in your life! If you like to kick up your heels and laugh, look for a fun exercise program such as roller skating, mountain biking, or a lively dance class. If, however, you're a no-nonsense kind of exerciser, try

an activity such as stationary biking, rowing, or using a stair climber.

8. *Competitiveness*. Does competition get you charged up, or does it discourage you from trying a new activity? Those motivated by competition thrive on winning a tennis match in the final set or kicking the crucial soccer goal. However, competition-shy folks do better with solo sports such as jumping rope, running, and biking.

9. *A homebody or an outdoorsy type.* Are your leanings more toward home, the health club, or the great outdoors? If you are a homebody by nature, you'll be more inclined to exercise with a stationary bicycle, slider, or workout videotapes—or even a personal trainer—in your home. Outdoorsy types need fresh air to stay motivated, and do best with walking, bicycling, canoeing, or cross-country skiing. People who prefer an indoor environment but haven't the space or discipline to work out at home may be more apt to start—and stick with—a fitness program by purchasing a health-club membership. (It's best to find a gym near your home or job; if getting to your club is inconvenient, you probably won't go.)

10. *A need to target specific body areas.* It's important to know your physical goals before choosing an exercise program. Yoga, tai chi, and water aerobics are ideal for anyone suffering back or neck pain, because they strengthen muscles without strain. (Of course, check with your doctor before starting an exercise program, and tell your instructor about any physical limitations.) If you're interested in strengthening and toning, you'll enjoy free weights, weight machines, or rubber-band classes (in which they pull large stretchy bands for resistance training). Those geared more toward cardiovascular workouts do best with lap swimming

(also easy on the joints), treadmills, and step aerobics. If you can combine strengthening and aerobic workouts, however, you'll be doing your body a very big favor. Research shows that combining these two elements (alternating aerobic-type activities with light weights, for instance) is the most efficient route to overall fitness.

11. *A morning or an evening person.* You're more likely to exercise if you capitalize on your body's natural energy cycles. Morning people do best exercising before work, when their energy levels are highest. Afternoon types can schedule lunch-hour walks or runs, or trips to the gym. Night owls need after-hours exercise settings, such as an indoor lap pool, a lightened tennis court, or a home exercise machine.

Procrastination: A Major Exercise Block

Many people put off exercising due to unrealistic expectations or false beliefs, which block their motivation. Sometimes, it's as obvious as the aversion someone developed to their high school physical education teacher. Other people who procrastinate fall into six general categories:

1. *The Preparer.* This person says, "I'll start exercising when…" or "I'll start going to aerobics class again when my friends join, too." Encouragement from friends and family is great, but most people need to look within themselves to start a lifetime of fitness.

    To prepare for a real workout properly, write down your exercise schedule on your calendar, just as you do with your other important appointments. Design a realistic schedule and then stick to it. Never cancel your exercise session—only reschedule it within the same day.

2. *The Shooting Star.* This overachiever dives into a new regimen wholeheartedly and often ends up overdoing it. This all-or-nothing fitness buff starts as a weekend warrior, and goes for a maximum burn in a minimum time, usually resulting in soreness or injury. The "bad back" or "bum knee" excuses then lead to avoiding the gym again until injuries heal. The Shooting Star may miss a few workouts and say, "I skipped a week of exercise, so I may as well give up."

3. *The Procrastinator.* "Should I exercise, or should I just wait until I feel 100 percent?" is the most familiar refrain from Procrastinators. Of course, anytime you allow yourself to even consider this question, the answer is invariably, "I don't have time (energy, patience, etc.) to exercise today."

4. *The Impatient Exerciser.* This person expects to see immediate weight loss and increased body tone after the first week! Disappointment accompanies the realization that working out requires slow, steady commitment in order to achieve relative gains. This person benefits from focusing on other rewards associated with exercise, such as stress management and improved energy levels.

5. *The Lifestyler.* This addictive personality tends to abuse alcohol, caffeine, and/or cigarettes, and often suffers from lack of sleep and general lethargy. The Lifestyler has an all-or-nothing approach to exercising. Like the Shooting Star, Lifestylers dive headfirst into a new workout program. However, their body's low energy levels, painful hangovers, or smoking-related problems will soon become their excuse for opting out of exercise.

6. *The Thrill Seeker.* A short attention span defines this personality type, along with a crammed schedule, and unrealis-

tic expectations that exercise is fun. Thrill Seekers often jump from one sport to another looking for adventure; they don't understand the importance of exercising to increase cardio-vascular capacity, flexibility, or muscular strength (that's too boring). What they crave is pure pleasure.

Time Strategies

During the times when you feel too busy, rushed, or tired to exercise, use these "tricks" to help pump up your motivation:

1. *See exercise as NON-optional.* The minute we allow our-selves to argue ("Do I have time to exercise, or don't I?"), we increase the odds of a sedentary lifestyle. Would you go to work in your pajamas and say, "I didn't have time to get dressed today"? Would you skip brushing your teeth because you're too tired? Of course not!

   People make time and find time for their priorities. Make exercise your priority, and then stick to your guns to make sure it happens. The good news is that you'll actually have more time and energy after a workout.

2. *Pair exercise with something really enjoyable.* Thrill Seekers, discussed above, need to add fun to their workouts since ex-ercise isn't always a pleasurable activity. Use a new book or magazine as a reward when you start walking on a treadmill, or after a really hard workout. Get through your toughest weightlifting routine by listening to a favorite tape or radio program. Put some money in a jar to save toward a special noncaloric treat after every workout. This way, you pair plea-sure and reward with exercise. For me, the benefits of exer-cise come after I'm through working out. I don't particularly care to exercise, but I'm always glad afterwards that I have!

3. *Do the "15-minute trick."* Here's another great motivator for The Preparer and The Procrastinator. Tell yourself, "I'll only work out for 15 minutes. If I feel like stopping at the end of those 15 minutes, I will." Nine times out of ten, you'll keep going once you've already donned clothes and driven to the gym.

4. *Take advantage of spare moments.* Fitness doesn't require hours and hours at the gym. The old "no pain, no gain" philosophy went out the window many years ago. You can achieve a toned, fit body with mini-workouts throughout the day. You can also perform stretches and calisthenics while engaging in another chore. For instance, do leg lifts while washing the dishes or putting on your makeup. Do deep knee bends when vacuuming the living room. Do stomach crunches while you're on hold on the telephone.

5. *Set realistic short-term goals.* The Impatient Exerciser and The Shooting Star abandon exercise programs when they don't see immediate results. It's important to approach exercise with realistic goals in mind. You will lose weight, change your body shape, and feel better—but not in one or two days. New exercisers may have to wait two weeks before noticing any results. If you're working out at a gym, yoga studio, or with a personal trainer, be sure and lean on these professionals if you ever feel discouraged. They will help you identify the progress you have already made, and pinpoint what you can expect in the future.

6. *Exercise on your way home.* Break up your commute with a stop at the gym, and you'll avoid heavy traffic and relieve the day's stress. Helpful hint: keep your gym bag, workout clothes, and shoes in your car at all times.

7. *Exercise with your family.* There are many ways to involve children and romantic partners into your exercise plans. For instance:

— Walk, jog, or roller skate while pushing a stroller.

— Bicycle with your young child in a bicycle seat, or accompany your older children on their own bicycles.

— Use a stationary bicycle or other exercise equipment in front of the television as you watch with your family.

— Many sport clubs offer babysitting services and/or children's workout rooms. Shop around, because this one feature may determine whether or not you make the effort to exercise.

— Join an athletic team, such as softball or volleyball, where families usually congregate. Check with your community parks and recreation department for information.

— Try a new sport as a family. Kayaking, horseback riding, and mountain climbing make excellent outings for families with older children.

— Hiking is a perfect way to enjoy a family outing, get plenty of exercise, fresh air, and take in the beauty of nature. Pack a healthful picnic, and voilà—you've got everything you need.

— Go for a family walk. Walking is excellent for toning leg muscles and burning calories, PLUS it encourages heart-to-heart discussions with family members.

— Consider taking a dance-style exercise class with one or more of your children. Ballet, country-and-western dance, tap dance, modern dance, or Jazzercize classes are wonderful exercises suitable for almost all ages.

— Learn an Eastern exercise together. Tai chi or martial arts provide excellent workouts, combined with lessons on balance, centering, breathwork, and other elements of serenity and poise.

Exercise is one of the most worthwhile investments of your time and energy, *especially* if you are juggling a heavy work and home schedule! When you involve your family in your fitness program, you teach them valuable ways to deal with their own stress. And the greatest benefit of all is that you won't have to sacrifice time together to get your own fitness needs met.

Points to Remember

* If exercise bores you, it's probably because your workout program doesn't fit your personality or lifestyle.

* View exercise as non-optional, and schedule a realistic exercise program into your week. Then stick to it, no matter what.

* If family concerns keep you from exercising, look for ways to work out *with* your family.

* Exercise gives you a large boost of energy, resulting in more productive hours during the day.

146

MAKING TIME FOR LOVE

"Love reckons hours for months, and days for years;
and every little absence is an age."

—JOHN DRYDEN (1631–1700),
ENGLISH AUTHOR

L ove comes in many forms, including romantic love, parent-
child love, love of friends, and the relationship you have
with your own self. I've yet to meet a man or woman who
said that he or she didn't want to have a love relationship. Yet many
people complain to me that they've given up hope of finding a suitable partner. Others say they don't have enough time to enjoy their
kids, marriage, or friends. Many people don't take time to renew
themselves with a few minutes spent alone.

In this chapter, we'll focus on the second tip of the life area
triangle—love. Let's examine ways to feel more energy in our relationships and for making the most of the time spent with our
loved ones.

Juggling Family and Work

Earlier, I suggested that you hold positive thoughts about your
schedule, to heal any sense of being overscheduled or rushed. If you
constantly think, "I don't have enough time," "No one supports my
efforts," or "How will I possibly get everything done," you will al-

ways have a negative outcome. These thoughts lower self-esteem, lessen energy, and discourage creative ideas.

Of course you don't want those results, so let's look at the situation in a different way! Visualize and focus upon what you *do* want, instead of what you *don't* want. Affirm to yourself:

+ I have unlimited energy, since I am made in the image and likeness of my Creator, who is pure energy.
+ Other people naturally and happily say "yes" in response to my requests for help.
+ Strong people, like me, delegate work accordingly.
+ I have enough time to accomplish all my desires.
+ I deserve to rest and take time out whenever necessary.
+ My children benefit when I enlist their help around the house.
+ My spouse pitches in around the house and gladly agrees to my requests for help.
+ I am lovable for who I am on the inside, not for what I do on the outside.
+ I choose to say "no" when I want to.
+ I let go of things and events that are out of my control.
+ I am not responsible for everything in the world around me.
+ I am a winner!

More Time for Us!

Many couples feel squeezed for time, rather than squeezed by a hug from one another. They procrastinate sharing romantic moments because they think, "Romance takes a lot of time. I'll wait until my schedule is more free. Then I'll enjoy romance with my sweetie." Unfortunately, by delaying the practice of sharing romance, couples soon find that warmth and passion have disappeared from the relationship. Many couples give their house plants more time and attention than they do their own relationships! We'd never expect a philodendron to thrive without water, but somehow our marriages are supposed to grow and flourish without any time or attention.

Fortunately, romance doesn't have to take a lot of time or involve effort. In fact, I define romance as "fun." While we usually think of romance as being spontaneous, the irony is that a little planning is necessary to guarantee a steady flow of warmth. It's important that you don't wait until your partner "goes first," though. Romantic standoffs ("I'll be romantic, but he has to start things off!") are a guaranteed route to a chilly relationship. One partner can single-handedly get the romantic ball rolling. So, practice one of these tips for 30 days, and you'll feel a remarkable warming trend in your relationship.

— *Celebrate your daily reunion.* The first five minutes that you and your honey see one another at the end of the day is crucial to setting the tone for the rest of your evening together. When you reunite after work, commit to focusing on one another exclusively. Don't open the mail or check the answering machine. Send the kids to their room for five minutes. Then sit on the sofa with your sweetheart, and simply hold one another. Maybe give one another a neck or a foot rub to alleviate the day's stress and to express mutual caring and affection. This five-minute ritual reminds a couple that "we're a united team." Bonded couples are less apt to let little things get on their nerves, which can result in time-wasting, energy-burning arguments.

— *Help your spouse help YOU!* Nothing kills romance faster than resentment, and many women feel steamed that their hubbies aren't pitching in around the home. A 1993 Families and Work Institute study found that men think they are doing more housework than they really are (43 percent of dual-income husbands said they were doing half the housework, while only 19 percent of dual-income wives felt that their husbands pitched in on a 50-50 basis). Women are usually more nurturing than men, so females usually notice when another person needs assistance. Men aren't as biologically or socially conditioned to look for signs that someone needs help; they usually have to be told or asked to help. *Bottom line*: women usually need to clearly request specific help around the home. Talk to your partner, and share your frustrations before they get the better of you and your relationship. Then hand him a list of ten things you'd like help with around the house.

— *Make dinnertime special.* Dinner is an opportunity for busy couples to share one-on-one time together, so make it a tranquil experience. My studies show that both men and women love candlelight dinners and consider them highly romantic. Buy fresh flowers at the grocery store or florist to add ambiance to your dinner table. Turn off the television or radio, and play some soft music (preferably a CD or cassette to avoid listening to commercials and news reports on the radio). Dim the lights, light the candles, and enjoy a relaxing meal together. Children are calmed by the flickering glow of candles, so don't hesitate to use them during family meals, too.

— *Surprise one another.* Romance doesn't have to take a lot of time. Little surprises do a lot to pleasantly shake up the energy in a relationship. Hide little love notes around the house in surprising places, such as under the pillow, in the medicine cabinet, or in the cereal box. Have a treasure hunt: hide a token gift, and put clues around your home leading to the "buried treasure." Is there an item that your sweetheart has been searching high and low for? Locate and buy the item, and you'll be your sweetie's hero or heroine!

— *Practice random acts of thoughtfulness.* Put out your honey's vitamins in the morning. Set the VCR to record your partner's favorite television show. Buy your road-weary sweetheart a commuter-style coffee mug. Buy or make his or her favorite dessert. Draw a bubble bath for both of you to share, or just for your partner to enjoy as you rub his or her back.

— *Turn ordinary moments into extraordinary moments.* Who says romance is reserved for faraway places such as exotic vacation spots, fancy restaurants, or resort hotels? Most two-career couples spend evenings at home in front of the television. So, snuggle up with one another, and hold hands like you did on your first movie date together. Pop some popcorn and toast your love with a special drink. Give each other foot rubs.

— *Plan to go out on a "date" tonight.* Once couples become a steady item, they often stop dating. This is a big mistake— long-term marrieds, newlyweds, and couples with young children—all need to date. One happy couple I know who are parents of two young children have dated every Friday night of their 14-year marriage. They take weekly turns planning the date, and they rigorously adhere to their date nights. As English playwright William Congreve wrote in the 1700s, *"Courtship is to marriage as a very witty prologue is to a very dull play."*

Time Savers for Busy Parents

Parents of young children constantly ask me for ideas on how to achieve their goals without sacrificing important family time. These parents feel trapped between the desire to improve their lives, and real responsibilities toward their children. At times, a parent may wrestle with impossible choices about how to spend his or her time.

Studies show how little time families actually spend talking with one another. A 1994 Angus Reid poll found that television watching was the main activity (average of 6.3 hours per week) parents spent with their children. Parent-child activities such as reading to one another or helping with homework received a mere 2.1 hours per week.

Everyone knows that a happy, fulfilled parent makes a better parent. But the parent doesn't want to spend so much time in self-fulfilling practices as to injure his or her child's mental or physical health! The Angus Reid poll found that 64 percent of dual-career parents felt their families received inadequate time and attention. Fortunately, there are ways to streamline a schedule. As the mother of two boys who are now grown, here are a few suggestions to help you:

— *Develop and adhere to routines.* Children adapt to, and even appreciate, routines. It helps them organize their thoughts and to know what to expect. So have a family meeting, and decide, for example, that Saturday is laundry day, Monday and Thursday are grocery shopping days, Sunday is family day, and so on.

Discuss and stick to daily routines, as well. Teach children how to schedule their morning time, from laying out clothes the night before, to creating a routine for showering, dressing, eating breakfast, and remembering to take their homework to school. Have them take control of evening hours, as well, by knowing "homework needs to be done by 7:30, bath time is at 8:00, brush teeth and have pajamas on by 8:30; lights out and quiet by 9:00." Routines help give you an interruption-free evening, precluding problems with children who rebel against performing their expected duties.

— *Assign chores to each family member, and post a list on the refrigerator.* When family members know exactly what is expected of them, arguments and misunderstandings are avoided.

Many women feel they are expected to do it all, but often they are not delegating tasks to the men and children of the household. Instead of complaining (which drains energy and is time-consuming), a woman must assertively outline what she expects from her family.

So, have a family meeting and discuss what household chores need to be done, by whom, and how often. Again, develop a routine. Billy feeds the dog when he gets home from school, Rachel sets the table at 6:00 P.M., Dad puts out the trash cans on Sunday night. Write down the chore assignments, along with one week's worth of spaces for checking the chore's completion, and post the list where it will be seen by all.

— *Place an out-basket by the door.* Time is precious, and no one can afford to make trips home to retrieve a forgotten item. Have family members get in the habit of placing outgoing items (homework, umbrellas, briefcase, keys, letters, library books, airline tickets, etc.) near the doorway, where they're most apt to see them..

— *Act, don't react.* Don't let family crises pull you from your priorities. If the kids are arguing during the 30 minutes you've set aside to practice your yoga or write your novel, don't be distracted from the task at hand. With the exception of a true emergency, don't allow family chaos to interfere with your dedication to your dream. Believe me, your children will notice, and model themselves after your behavior. You're doing them a favor by exemplifying a "first things first" policy.

— *Don't expect perfection.* Don't bog down your schedule and

emotions by expecting unimportant tasks to be perfectly per-
formed. After all, does it really matter if there's dust under
the refrigerator, or the laundry isn't perfectly folded? Your
children may not be adept at sweeping the floor, but don't
sweat it if they miss a crumb or two. Adopt a policy of
"good enough is good enough" with your third-order priorities. Save perfectionism for things that *really* matter.

— *Get outside help.* Working moms, even those who work from
home, benefit greatly from hiring a housekeeping service.
Have these invaluable helpers come in once or twice a month
and do heavy-duty cleaning. For around $50, you can leave
your worries about dust under the counters and grime in the
sinks behind you. Many women's incomes rise once they are
relieved of the time-consuming burden of cleaning showers
and ovens. See if there's some nonessential item you can cut
from your budget to pay for housecleaning help. Family
members can still be assigned small daily chores to maintain
a tidy home between professional cleanings.

— *Streamline your schedule.* Instead of going grocery shopping
on your way home from work every evening, you'll save
hours and hours by only shopping once a week. Put an ice
chest in your car to keep perishables fresh during long shopping expeditions. Shop at off-peak times and days to avoid
long lines. Supplement your major weekly shopping venture
with occasional stops at small neighborhood stores for fresh
milk and meats (where such items are high quality and value
priced). Combine your shopping outings so you can hit the
department store, supermarket, and hairdresser all on the
same day. Don't hesitate to ask your spouse or teenage children to pick up your dry cleaning or a gallon of milk on their
way home. Develop a rotating menu—pasta on Monday,
chicken on Tuesday, burgers on Wednesday, and so on—so

you can shop more efficiently and won't have to wrack your brain for recipe ideas.

— *Make waiting time count.* You're at the dentist's office, waiting while your children's teeth are being examined. Instead of flipping through an old *Field and Stream*, take advantage of the free time. Carry a small notepad in your purse so you can jot down short hello's or thank you's to out-of-town friends. Keep an interesting book or magazine in your car at all times. When you know you'll be waiting in line or will be sitting in a waiting room, you'll have something enjoyable to read.

— *Set aside family time.* After all, it's one of the main reasons we work so hard! As with any relationship, it's important to plan time together. Make time for regular family days, such as Sundays, where everybody sets aside time to be together. Then go to the park or a lake and enjoy a picnic together. Go to church, and worship together. See a movie matinee. Buy a new puppy or kitty. Fly kites, swing on swings, rent a boat. The *what* doesn't matter...as much as the fact that you're all spending time together.

— *Question authority.* Your boss asks you to work overtime the night of your child's school play. Your manager suggests that you head a new committee that requires you to travel seven days a month. Your personnel manager informs you that the company will cease paying for family member health insurance. What do you do? Although jobs seem to be precious and few, your priority is your family. Talk with your boss about your concerns regarding spending time away from your family. Don't automatically say "yes" to requests that pull you away from your loved ones. Many companies offer some type of child care; perhaps it's time to shop around the job market for a company that is family-friendly.

— *Involve your family in your personal routines.* Who says that self-care has to be a solo venture? Invite your children to join you for a relaxing walk or bicycle ride around the block. Play tennis together. Take your son or daughter to an afternoon tea or social event. Enroll in a fun adult-school class, such as photography, tai chi, or acting, with your teenager. Join a gym that offers babysitting services and/or children's activities. Bring your kids to the office when you have to work on Saturdays. Ask your family to help you compose your new ad campaign. Whatever it is you need to do for yourself, see if you can involve your family in the project. Make every moment count!

— *Praise your children's efforts.* Everyone needs pats on the back and appreciation. So when the kids pitch in with kitchen clean-ups and such, loudly praise their efforts. A smile or a thank you encourages your child to help you in the future.

— *Reward yourselves.* You all work hard, so be sure and treat yourselves. Take the family out for ice cream, a movie, or a sporting event. Declare that you are celebrating the fact that you are a family. Live it up in celebration of Mom's new promotion, or Johnny's baseball victory. Your family will feel like a winning team!

— *Stop outside interruptions and interferences.* Don't let a phone call or unexpected visitor keep you from enjoying time with your children! Have the answering machine pick up your calls, and tell the uninvited guests that you're happy to see them, but you're all tied up at the moment so you'll have to plan to see them sometime in the future. Openly admit to phone callers that your family time is a high priority that you need to attend to at the moment. They'll respect you for it!

— *Create alone time for you and your partner.* Most parents won't be surprised by the results of a 1993 Massachusetts Mutual Life Insurance survey: Moms and Dads want time to themselves! Seventy-five percent of working mothers, 65 percent of nonworking mothers, and 33 percent of working fathers said they didn't have enough free time away from the children.

When my brother and I were small, my parents would often retreat into their master bedroom and put up a "Do Not Disturb" sign on their door. We kids didn't think twice about it, but as an adult, I have immense respect for the fact that my parents created time alone for themselves. You might swap babysitting services with friends, and adhere to a weekly date with just the two of you alone. Keep your marriage a high priority, and the kids will benefit in the long and short run.

— *Get organized.* Your home, like your office, needs efficient management to run smoothly. Make it easy on yourself by organizing your home space in ways that save everyone time and aggravation. Once a year, clean out the closets and re-arrange items in your home so they are organized in user-friendly ways. Misplaced items can become stressful time-wasters. Hang a large calendar on your kitchen wall to keep track of personal and family activities. Post a combination chalk/bulletin board (with plenty of chalk and push pins!) where family members can scribble notes to one another.

— *Hold regular family meetings.* Once or twice a month, plan to spend a few hours together discussing family goals, problems, chores, vacations, and mutual activities. Take turns leading the meeting and keeping minutes. Children will learn the art of effective communicating during meetings—a valuable skill for their adult careers. Make ground rules for family meetings, such as no name-calling, interrupting, tardiness, or absences.

— *Plan ahead.* Not only will your schedule be more streamlined, but you'll also be setting an example for your children when you implement sound time-management strategies into your daily life. For example, is your daughter planning to attend a friend's birthday party next month? Purchase the birthday gift during your next shopping excursion to avoid a last-minute scramble. Daily routines can be planned ahead, as well: if your son's bedtime is 8:00, have him plan to have homework done by 7:00 P.M., his toys put away, and his next-day clothes laid out by 7:30. That way, he and you can enjoy a half hour together reading stories or talking before bedtime.

— *Capitalize on unplanned time.* Do you have 15 minutes to spare before it's time to leave for work? Grab your child and share a morning hot cocoa together. Do the spaghetti noodles need to simmer for five more minutes before they're ready to eat? Spend that five minutes playing with your son or daughter on the floor. A few minutes here and there add up to special moments with your child. Don't wait until that mythical day in the future when you'll "have more time"! Create shared moments with your family member through little five-, ten-, or fifteen-minute increments.

How to Have More Time for You!

In one of singer Whitney Houston's most popular songs, she tells of how she found the greatest love of all right inside of her. Well, that sentiment is absolutely right! Let's not forget one of our most important love relationships: the one we have with ourselves. Whether you live alone, with one person, or with a large family, you still need time for yourself. But hectic days and multiple responsibilities can make alone time seem like an impossible dream. Here are some ways to carve out moments for yourself. You'll feel revived and renewed by implementing these suggestions, which ultimately help all of your other relationships, as well.

1. Just do it! Don't wait for your family to notice that you need time by yourself. That time may never come! Instead, schedule 30 minutes a day to spend time alone. Put a "Do Not Disturb" sign on your bedroom door. Or pay a responsible neighborhood teen a few dollars to watch your kids for an hour, and instruct her not to interrupt you.

2. Then, take a nap, read a novel, or daydream. Soak in a bubble bath, complete with scented candles around the tub. Go for a nature walk, see that romantic comedy movie no one else wants to watch, or go shopping for a special treat. Get a massage, pedicure, or facial. Meditate, pray, or stretch. Paint a watercolor portrait of your favorite landscape while listening to classical music. Write poetry, walk barefoot in the grass, play a guitar.

The main thing is to *just do it*—create one half hour or more just for yourself, even if it means having to cut back on television viewing or talking with friends on the phone. Remember: you're worth it!

Romance Surrounds You

Busy singles, especially single parents, often struggle to make time to meet new people and date. How are you supposed to help your son do his homework, take your daughter to swimming lessons, fix dinner, and go on a date—all in the same evening?

Some singles have simply given up, or have put their love lives on hold until their children are older. Others have intermittent love lives, and only date occasionally. But many singles crave the romance and companionship of a steady relationship. However, their tight schedules keep them out of the dating scene.

Here are some suggestions, culled from my own experiences as a single mother, and from working with single counseling clients and workshop attendees for the past dozen years:

1. *Make your life gracious and romantic, now.* It's a mistake to delay the enjoyment of life while you wait to be in a relationship. Romance is a state of mind, and you deserve to enjoy its pleasant feelings every day—with or without a partner. Plus, anything that boosts your mood also boosts your opportunities to meet Mr. or Ms. Right. We're naturally more friendly, outgoing, and attractive when we're in a good mood!

   So, create a romantic atmosphere at your home with a fresh flower bouquet and candles. Soak in a hot bubble bath surrounded by candles, and accompanied by soft music, great reading material, and a refreshing drink. Watch a romantic movie; sway to classical music; turn your bedroom into a comfortable retreat stuffed with pillows, fresh linens, and flowers. Children are calmed by candlelight and soft music, so don't hesitate to engage in romantic activities just because the kids are around.

2. *Go places.* You can't meet the man or woman of your dreams while holed up alone at home (with the exception of a pizza delivery person). You also don't want to put your life on hold waiting for a relationship to make you feel complete. That's why evening classes and self-improvement activities are perfect: they get you out of the house where you can meet new people, and they help enrich your life as well.

Most communities have adult education centers offering interesting evening and weekend classes. What a perfect way to learn something new and make new friends! Many classes allow or encourage older children to participate, so don't feel you have to take time away from your family to enjoy an evening out.

Spiritual growth groups are another way to enjoy yourself and meet friends. *A Course in Miracles* study groups, meditation or yoga classes, and psychic development training are groups that stimulate self-growth in more ways than one. Call your local metaphysical book store for information on groups in your area.

3. *Be approachable.* Eligible dating and marriage partners are *everywhere* in great abundance! I can't help but chuckle when my workshop attendees complain that there are "no good single people anywhere." These are usually the same people who complain that "there are too many people on the road," or "the crowds at the bank, post office, store, and so on are overwhelming!" Those crowds are chock-full of potential dating partners. But we often overlook these natural sources of eligible dates because we're in a rush, or assume that romance only happens in "date-like" places.

Be open to meeting potential dates in ordinary places that you frequent during your busy week: the grocery store, dry cleaners, library, post office, frozen yogurt shop, video rental store, bank, commuter bus or train, health club, veterinarian's office, or gas station. When you're out, make friendly eye contact with other people. Wear or carry something that will start a conversation: an eye-catching pin, a slogan-bearing shirt, a book, a piece of sporting equipment, or a pet. If someone smiles at you, say "Hi" and then let nature take its course. Assume the best when talking to a new person ("I naturally make friends," "People always like me") so you'll radiate a positive attitude. Focus on having fun, and you'll reduce self-conscious worries.

4. *Hang out with friends*. Studies show that most people are introduced to their future spouse through friends. After all, we share similar values with our friends. So, it makes sense that our friends' friends will also share our values—a key element in successful love relationships.

   Busy people don't always have much time for friendships. No problem! You can streamline your social life by suggesting a potluck dinner or cocktail party. If everybody brings a dish or drink, then nobody needs to work too hard to create a nice evening together. Other ideas include a group bicycle ride, a volleyball or softball game, a shared vacation retreat, or a semi-monthly discussion group. You can catch up with your friends and meet *their* single friends without much time or trouble. Be sure and include everyone's children in these events.

5. *Decide what you want*. In Chapter 3, I discuss how I used visualization and affirmations to find Michael, the man of my dreams. I wrote a detailed description of every quality important to me in a mate. That way, instead of dating whatever man happened to drift into my life (and then attempting to change him into the man I really wanted), I started with a man who suited me. This proactive method of dating has turned out to be so much more satisfying than my old, reactive style!

   My suggestion is that you clarify the precise characteristics you desire in a mate. You already know which habits you would never put up with (such as dishonesty, infidelity, abusiveness, etc.). So, this is your chance to really pinpoint what you *do* want! Write down all the qualities of your dream mate. But leave out the items you honestly don't care about (such as whether the person has brown or blue eyes, etc.).

   Once you're done with your list, then:

6. *Call upon Cupid.* The little winged cherub really does exist in
    the form of inner and spiritual assistance. Be determined to
    meet your right partner, and pray for spiritual guidance. Vi-
    sualize Cupid flying all around and then finding your perfect
    mate for you. See Cupid arranging a series of coincidences that
    culminates in the two of you meeting. Pay attention to any gut
    feelings or hunches that lead you to meet Mr. or Ms. Right.
    Then obey those instincts (as I did, thank goodness!) even if
    they seem silly or illogical. Trust Cupid to make the impos-
    sible...possible!

Healing Your Love Life

Many of my clients are married women, and although they don't
come to me initially for marital problems, the subject often
arises. I trained in traditional psychotherapeutic marriage, family,
and child work. I took all the necessary courses for licensure as a
marriage counselor. Yet, for all my traditional training, I teach my
clients to use spiritual healing practices to heal their love-life problems. This involves focusing on the spiritual truth of your loved
one, and refusing to see anything but their true state of a perfect
being, wholly made of God's love and wisdom. This person is ca-
pable of only love and loving behavior, and anything else that appears to be the case is just an illusion.

Whatever you focus upon *always* enlarges. If you concentrate on
the true, loving nature of each person, their loving behavior will increase. If, however, you do what traditional psychology recom-
mends—and analyze what is wrong with that person or with your
relationship—then don't be surprised if the problem grows worse!

This is one reason why I suggest that my clients avoid having
lengthy discussions with their friends or group therapy mates about
their "relationship problems." Without mental illness, abuse, or sub-
stance addictions, almost all relationship issues (even those just
named) respond beautifully to spiritual healing. See only the love

within your partner, and that is what you'll get back. The more intently and purely your focus is upon your partner's true nature, the more quickly you'll see his or her behavior change toward you. It's literally *loving the hell* out of someone!

Through spiritual healing, surliness turns to warmth, inexpressiveness turns to open communication, and distant people draw closer. Everyone can sense when they are appreciated and loved, and when you shine your beam of love upon your partner, you can melt an iceberg in his or her heart. You, too, will feel more loving and closer to your partner and will find yourself falling in love all over again. You'll see miraculous results by applying spiritual treatment. Love never fails!

Healing Conflicts

Needless arguments are a colossal waste of time and energy. There is all that physical exertion and adrenaline that builds up from getting so upset. And, you become further drained as you replay the argument over and over again in your mind, searching for tidbits of evidence that the other person is to blame. Next, you worry and wonder about which options to take. Should you call off the relationship? Should you talk it out and make up? What a draining experience!

There is a better way to handle such situations! Take Sheila, for instance:

> Sheila and Mark were married for 22 years and jointly owned and operated an insurance agency. Mark enjoyed selling insurance immensely, and he made a great income. Sheila, however, didn't like being the office bookkeeper at all. Her heart pulled her toward more artistic, creative employment. But how was she supposed to have time to learn a new craft with her full-time work and tight family schedule?

Sheila approached Mark several times with the idea of hiring a bookkeeper to take her place, and the couple always ended up arguing. I asked Sheila to describe her mental frame of mind upon talking to Mark about her quandary. It did not surprise me to learn that Sheila expected Mark to be and act disagreeable, since that was the result she was getting from him.

I asked Sheila to hold a mental image of her and Mark lovingly agreeing that hiring a bookkeeper made good personal and financial sense for the couple. She pictured Mark smiling and hugging her, and readily agreeing to her request. "But he's already told me 'no' three times," she protested, when I asked her to approach Mark another time.

"He will say 'no' a fourth time if that's what you expect," I counseled her. "Think about what you want, not about what you don't want."

Sheila agreed to talk to Mark while holding firm expectations of a positive outcome. She called me the next day with breathless amazement in her voice. "It worked!" she practically shouted into the phone. "Mark said 'yes,' just as I'd imagined." I hung up the phone after our conversation, pleased but not surprised by Sheila's experience.

You, too, can create whatever scenarios you want with your loved ones through your positive expectations. I can't emphasize this point enough:

> *Focus upon what you want,*
> *not upon what you don't want.*

Healing Parent-Child Relationships

Just as knowing the truth about your spouse or lover heals the relationship, so too does this process work beautifully between a parent and a child.

My client, Janice, was extremely worried about her teenage daughter, Ashley. "She is so hard to get along with lately," Janice told me. "Ashley's also secretive, bossy, and disrespectful. The more I confront her, the worse it seems to get. Not only that, but I just found a pamphlet in her room that makes me think Ashley is going to join a cult. Help! What can I do?"

I offered various options to Janice, and she decided to use spiritual healing treatment. Every time she would look at, think about, or interact with, Ashley, Janice would know—absolutely know— that her teenage daughter was a holy, loving child of God. Janice would remember that God put Ashley into her life for a higher purpose and that Ashley was Janice's angelic messenger.

Within one week, the entire situation was completely healed and has held steady for almost one year now. Ashley rapidly responded to the spiritual treatment (as children usually do) by dropping her cold defensiveness and sarcastic attitude. Instead, she began spending more time with the family, and became the cooperative, loving daughter that Janice had visualized.

Spiritual healing works well with any relationship in your life, including relatives (deceased or alive), friends, co-workers, bosses, neighbors, store clerks...and even household pets!

POINTS TO REMEMBER

🐦 Romance doesn't have to take a lot of time. Small random acts of thoughtfulness, fun, and closeness save relationships and help couples avoid time-consuming conflicts.

🐦 Develop routines with your family to get chores assigned and accomplished. Stick to your priorities, and don't expect perfection when it comes to relatively unimportant chores.

🐦 Don't neglect your most important love relationship—the one you have with yourself. Take at least 30 minutes a day to be alone with yourself in a fun or relaxing way.

🐦 Even the busiest single person can enjoy romance, friendship, and a wonderful love life.

🐦 A focus on "what is wrong" in a relationship only makes things worse. Concentrate on what you *want* in your love life, not on what you don't want.

🐦 See the true, loving nature in your loved ones, and they will respond lovingly in return.

🐦 🐦 🐦

MORE TIME FOR YOUR CAREER AND FINANCES

"Great minds have purposes, others have wishes."
— WASHINGTON IRVING (1783–1859),
AMERICAN WRITER

Many people dream of changing or quitting their jobs, or of making more money. In a 1995 *Money* magazine poll, 65 percent of respondents said that they are working harder and longer hours compared to one year earlier, but making less money and taking shorter vacations. When a tight budget forces you to spend hours and hours at a dissatisfying job, how can you have enough time or energy to make changes in your career? This chapter focuses on the third tip of the life area triad—career and finances.

It's a very important life area, to be sure. Our earning power correlates to the amount of free time we enjoy, the quality of our health care or ability to pay for legal fees, and even the safety of the neighborhood in which we live or the car we drive! Money can literally spell life or death in certain situations.

With all its importance, it's no wonder that many people frantically worry about how to improve their financial lot. Still other people crave something even more valuable than money: a meaningful career. These days, many burnt-out workers are tempted to quit their jobs, sell everything, and live a simpler life.

The above-mentioned goals are understandable and achievable, though. Yet, they all require the same willingness to make time and commitments, just as is the case with the other two life areas of health and love.

Getting Over Money Guilt

It's so stressful to worry about money. It keeps people awake at night and leads to family discord. With this much impact upon our emotional and physical health, why do so many people believe it's wrong to want more money? In truth, I've found that while they'd like to be rich, most people are really after financial comfort and security. It's that wake-up-in-the-middle-of-the-night panic over how one will pay the credit card bills, groceries, rent or car payments that shortens lives and ruins health. Why would we feel guilty or wrong for wanting to eliminate that worrisome area of our lives?

Some people have told me that they think it's spiritually or morally "wrong" to want money. Yet, when I talk at length with these folks, I invariably find that they are obsessed with thoughts about money. They tend to focus all their money thoughts upon lack and fear. People with money troubles think about money more than any other group of people, and it's no wonder this is the case, because whatever you focus upon tends to become your physical reality. If you think about "a lack of money" all day long, what do you think your financial life will look like?

So, you see, thinking about money isn't the problem—it's worrying about it and/or irresponsibly using the money you have. My studies of world religions and motivational/success books have revealed a common thread of knowledge running through most of them:

Know that you deserve to have, and will always have, your every human need met. Do not worry or make yourself upset over your current financial conditions, or you risk losing your serenity and blocking the flow of greater good into your life. Force yourself, if you must, to have faith that your needs have always been met in the past, and they always will be met in the future. Pray and meditate on ideas for serving humanity, and when that wisdom comes to you, be sure and act upon it. The more you give to others, the more abundance will flow into your life. Always remember that God, not people or jobs, is your Source. If you count on Him to supply your needs, you will always be taken care of.

In Biblical times, they called silver coins "talents." It's an interesting term, considering the high value we place upon talent. Just look at any list of the highest paid and wealthiest people, and you'll usually find comedians and actors.

You have talents and unique gifts that you can exchange for silver talents—money.

Have you ever looked at the back of money and noticed all the spiritual symbolism? First, there's the pyramid, an ancient symbol of focused power and energy. Next, there is a third eye, or God-eye, the symbol of all-knowingness. And the term, "In God we trust," shows our surrender to divine will and our trust in spiritual fairness.

I believe that God simply wants us to trust that He will provide for us. He doesn't want us to suffer or go without any more than you'd want your own children to suffer. Let go of money guilt; it's a sign of distrust that will only block the happiness and comfort you were born to enjoy!

Three prosperity books that I highly recommend are *The Abundance Book,* by John Randolph Price; *The Trick to Money Is Having Some,* by Stuart Wilde; and *The Dynamic Laws of Prosperity,* by Catherine Ponder. These three books are excellent tools for developing a prosperity consciousness so that you can be free of money worries forever.

How to Make a Living Loving What You Do

One of the greatest tragedies I can think of is to work at a meaningless job. We trade our lives in return for a reward of money. Meaningful employment comes from enjoying what you do and feeling that you've made a positive difference in someone's life through your efforts.

Now, this doesn't mean that you have to save lives to have a job that counts. Not at all! There are many ways in which jobs positively influence the world, including:

— Jobs in the entertainment industry, which uplift people's spirits
— Service and health-care jobs that help people's lives run more smoothly
— Information distribution jobs, which alert people to important events, products, and data
— Support positions that create opportunities or products that people need

The specific type of work you're involved in isn't as important as two other considerations:

— *The interactions between you and other people.* We are here on earth for the primary purpose of living a life of pure love, free of judgment. Anytime you interact with another person, you have the opportunity for soul growth and healing by acting out of love. Every person we meet, whether a clergyperson, homeless man or woman, boss, co-worker, customer, or celebrity, is a brother or sister made by your Creator. All people are motivated by desires to give or to receive love. We remember these truths by surrendering unforgiveness and judgments about ourselves and others. As it says in *A Course in Miracles*, "When you meet anyone, remember it is a holy encounter."

— *Enjoying and appreciating the work that you do.* Your passions are your guide to discovering and living your purpose in life. Whatever activities you would choose to do in your free time, without being paid, are those that have been divinely inspired within you for the purpose of helping the world and providing for your material needs. My father, Bill Hannan, for example, turned his childhood hobby of building balsa wood model airplanes into his full-time career. He continues to writes books and sells plans for model airplanes, and he has always been fulfilled, as well as making a great income.

Just about any daily job can become more meaningful—and thus more enjoyable—by injecting some moments of warm human connectedness into the day. This may involve your taking the time to listen to a troubled co-worker, or going out of your way to assist a customer. It could mean locating a leak in the company's profit margin, or suggesting a new invention. Know that you can be creative and make each day of your work life count!

Becoming a Professional Healer

As part of this chapter on making your career meaningful, I'd like to discuss a unique phenomenon that I, along with many of my peers, have noticed. Many people that we have been in contact with recently have felt a "calling" to become healers. Almost as if a massive help wanted ad was being psychically transmitted, many individuals are feeling the urgency to do something to help the world.

My friends, peers, and clients who have heard or felt this calling have reacted in different ways. Some have felt distressed because they don't see themselves as qualified to perform any healing function. They may secretly hope that the pressure to perform a healing function will go away, but they usually find that it only increases. They also worry whether they can make a living performing a healing function. Still others have heeded the call and have enrolled in traditional and nontraditional healing instruction courses.

Since this phenomenon is being acknowledged by so many people simultaneously, it is something worth noting. I believe that there is a mass spiritual call for workers to help in healing some destructive and negative tendencies that are prevalent in today's world. Those people who are sensitive and attuned are hearing the call, because these are the necessary characteristics for being an effective healer.

Perhaps you, too, have felt the calling to perform a positive function in the world. If so, let me reassure you that it is wonderful that you were called! Please know that you would not have been called unless Spirit knew that you were qualified. In other words, there's no need for you to second-guess Spirit and question It with a, "Who, me? You're talking to me? I'm not qualified!" You've already gotten the job.

Author/lecturer Marianne Williamson likens these divine assignments to being a soldier in an army and following orders. We may not always have access to the big picture, and we may not always understand why we're assigned to perform this task or that. But what we are required to do is to follow our commander's orders. A good soldier doesn't argue with his leader and say that he isn't up to the assigned task. He or she just does it.

How to Be a Healer in Everyday Life

This call for healers does not necessarily mean that you should quit your day job and enroll full-time in acupuncture school or a counseling program. It only means that you are asked to incorporate healing practices into your daily activities. In other words, the role of healer doesn't necessarily have to become a full-time, salaried position. It just needs to be your full-time way of being.

Heeding the call to heal entails acting with kindness in all situations and looking for opportunities to teach others about the power of love and the limitations of guilt and fear. According to *A Course in Miracles*, teaching the importance of love is the best way to reinforce the lesson within ourselves.

Don't wait until you've mastered this topic before sharing it with others. Instead, teach what you want to truly learn. I'm not suggesting that you give lectures to your co-workers on the virtues of spirituality or love. Some of the best instruction occurs through example. For instance, you can best teach others about living a peaceful life by speaking and acting in a calm manner. You can impart your wisdom about loving behavior by exhibiting such actions yourself.

The most important component of the mass call for healers is this: do it now. We can all play a role in healing the world starting immediately. Your smile to another driver may start a chain reaction of kindness that could save someone's life on the road. Teaching someone about prosperity consciousness could inspire someone to leave behind a life of crime.

Know this, please: you are eminently qualified for the role you have been assigned. You deserve this success now. Any feelings you have about being inadequate or unqualified may actually turn into a self-fulfilling prophecy, as distrust in the healing powers of love can create unsatisfying or even negative results. Know that you are merely a conduit for the healing and loving powers of Spirit. All you need do is to practice loving behavior toward others in all your thoughts and deeds.

Nontraditional Healing Careers

If your gut feelings do direct you toward a salaried profession in the healing arts and sciences, there are many different ways to go about seeking one out. Just about any metaphysical bookstore carries a newsletter or monthly magazine that lists spiritual healing and alternative medicine training seminars. Many of these publications carry advertisements about healer certification courses. (Also, Hay House, my publisher, has information about Louise Hay's teacher-training courses. Feel free to write for information—the address can be found at the back of this book.)

I would call for detailed information about healing courses before jumping into them, though, especially if a sizable investment of money or time is required. Remember that anyone can offer a certificate in anything they want, but it doesn't mean it's a legitimate service or viable option for you. Ask the school or course leader for referrals to past attendees, and then use your gut feelings to discern the level of satisfaction that was realized (or not).

Time-Saving Strategies to Simplify Your Work Life

Whether or not you're planning on changing careers, you'll still want to make the most of every moment. After all, healing begins with our own lives! One way to feel more at peace throughout the day is by simplifying your schedule. You'll have a lot more time, energy, and enthusiasm by trimming the fat from your work schedule. Here are some tried-and-true reminders for ways to maximize your time, as well as some new twists on old ideas:

— *Capitalize on your energy cycles.* Are you a morning person or a night owl? Schedule your most important activities around your energy peaks. Our bodies go through circadium rhythms much like a rolling wave that constantly builds and crashes. The body temperature rises and falls throughout the day, with corresponding energy peaks and valleys. Most people experience optimal mental sharpness between 10:00 A.M. and noon, and then again between 3:00 and 4:00 P.M. The worst hours for mental alertness are between noon and 2:30 P.M., with the lowest valley being around 1:00 in the afternoon.

— *Take charge of interruptions.* A major study found that on average, half of each work day is wasted on unproductive conversations with co-workers and personal telephone calls. While it's fun and even relaxing to chat with other people, we pay dearly for overdoing it later. The stress of facing incomplete, overdue work projects drains our energy and robs us of personal free time. You wouldn't hand out $50 bills freely to everyone who asks you for money, would you? Well, then, place time interruptions in the same category. Discourage interruptions by:

- Standing up when someone walks in your office.
- Asking, "What can I do for you?" instead of "How are you?"
- Saying, "I'd love to talk to you, but I've got to get this project finished; how about scheduling some time together Wednesday at 2:00, or after work on Thursday?"
- Screening all telephone calls through a receptionist, voice mail, or an answering machine. On your answering machine message, request that callers "please leave a detailed message, including the best time" to reach you, so you can avoid playing telephone tag or making unnecessary phone calls to hear information that could be left on your recorder.

— *Don't try to do it all.* Yes, you are special, but specialness doesn't mean having to do it all. Easy does it! Avoid performing multiple activities at the same time, for example, driving a car while applying makeup and listening to a self-help audiocassette. It's better to make steady progress toward your goal, instead of burning yourself out by overdoing it. If you get overloaded with responsibilities, ask for help, and focus only on high-priority activities.

— *Separate urgent from vital. Urgent* means a sudden crisis, but *vital* means an essential priority. Don't let a crisis pull you away from a vital activity. Instead, let the fire of the crisis burn out on its own. All crises eventually resolve themselves one way or another, so remind yourself, "This too shall pass."

— *Put a price on your time.* Is your time worth $25, $50, or $100 an hour? Set your hourly rate, and then decide which tasks to handle and which to delegate based upon this price. For example, if your time is worth $50 an hour, why would you file correspondence when you can hire clerical help at $10 an hour? If you work at home and your hour is worth $75, why not hire a $20-an-hour housekeeper once a week to take over your cleaning chores?

— *Capitalize on bits and pieces of time.* It's amazing how much work can be accomplished in five- or ten-minute increments! If possible, carry a portion of your current project with you while running errands to work on while waiting in line or while your car is being washed. Catch up on your reading with audio books, which are available at any public library or bookstore. Use your lunch hour for pleasure reading, personal correspondence, or taking a college class (I got through Algebra 101 with a lunch-hour class at a campus near my office).

— *Vacuum your life.* There's incredible wisdom in the maxim, "Nature abhors a vacuum and rushes to fill it." It's true! Here's how to apply this wisdom to your practical, time-saving advantage:

- Donate unwanted items. Do you want new clothes, books, or furniture? Then clear out your old to make way for the new. Once you give away your unwanted items, you'll be amazed by how quickly replacements come your way in "coincidental" ways.
- Clear away unwanted tasks or duties. Does attending your social club feel more like a duty than a benefit?

Are you too busy to hold officership in your organization? If so, make room for new organizations and friendships that suit who you are today! Say "no" to requests for favors that don't fit your priorities or values. By creating a time vacuum, you'll attract opportunities that really excite you.

— *Be electronics-friendly.* Modern electronics are a double-edged sword: on the one hand, it's nice that pagers, faxes, and cellular phones give us freedom to travel away from the office. But they also mean we're always on-call. Take control of electronic equipment, instead of becoming its slave. For example, most cellular and pager services offer voice mails for a nominal charge. It's worth it, because you won't need to take every call that comes through. Use e-mail and faxes instead of lengthy telephone chats, and encourage your business associates to reply in the same time-saving manner.

— *Use mobile services.* You can take care of a manicure, haircut, massage, and psychotherapy appointment—right in your own office! Also, many dry cleaners offer mobile services, picking up and delivering clothing at your workplace

Cutting Stress from Your Commute

Driving to and from work requires a big chunk of time and energy for about 108 million Americans who commute daily. University of California researcher Dr. Raymond Novaco found a direct correlation between commute distance and increased blood pressure. Other factors linked to commuting probably won't surprise road warriors: impaired memory and concentration, relationship discord, and an intolerance for frustration. Many people arrive at work so pooped from their commute that their performance suffers, and ordinary tasks take inordinate amounts of time to complete. Dr. Novaco's research found that female executives were particularly prone to commuter stress, and take longer to shake off the stress of a long drive.

Fortunately, there are ways to relieve the stress of daily commuting:

TEN WAYS TO CUT COMMUTING STRESS

1. *Cocoon your car.* A peaceful, comfortable environment is essential to a tranquil commute:

    — Use fragrance. Potpourri in the ashtray, sachets over the air vent, air fresheners, and fresh flowers enhance your driving experience. Choose relaxing scents such as vanilla, or stimulating aromas such as cinnamon, peppermint, or eucalyptus.

    — Interact with your radio. Call your favorite station from your cell phone and join the conversation on a talk show, or request your favorite song on a music station.

    — Sit pretty. Buy a super-comfortable seat cushion or a heated seating pad that plugs into your cigarette lighter.

    — Fax machines, mini-refrigerators, cell phone voice mail, and television sets bring convenience to your automobile. The Campbell Soup Company even predicts that by the year 2000, one-quarter of all autos will be equipped with microwave ovens! Of course, utilizing some of the above items only works if you're a passenger in the vehicle and are not actually doing the driving!

    — Wear comfy sweats while driving. Change into your stiff business suit when you get to your office building.

2. *Know the roads.* Study a map, and figure out alternative routes to get to work. By doing so, when gridlock hits, you can jump off the nearest exit and drive the surface streets. Monotony is stressful, so purposely vary your commuting route on a regular basis, if possible.

3. *Carpool.* Although many people prefer to ride alone during commutes, University of California studies found that ride-sharing significantly lowers blood-pressure levels in commuters. Ride-sharers are also less likely to be bothered by traffic congestion or the commute distance.

4. *Plan ahead.* Get gas, cash, and other necessities on the weekend or after work. It's too stressful to race for supplies on the way in to the office. Keep paper towels and glass cleaner in your car so your windshield will stay easy-on-the-eyeballs clean. If you usually run ten minutes late for appointments, set your watch ahead so you'll be on time.

5. *Stretch and get out.* Sitting in one position during a long commute is a sure-fire way to experience back pain and sore muscles. It's important to shift your body weight and leg positions every 10 or 15 minutes. Better yet, pull off the road, get out of your car, and s-t-r-e-t-c-h. The three to five minutes involved is time well invested.

6. *Drive the speed limit.* Studies show that speeding a mere ten miles over the limit significantly increases heart rate and blood pressure. Stick to the slow lane, and let the hotheads pass you by.

7. *Seek alternatives.* Discuss flex time or telecommuting possibilities with your employer. If you live close enough to work, consider riding a bicycle for a healthful commuting al-

ternative. Investigate public transportation options, including company van-pools, trains, subways, and public buses. Consider moving closer to work, or finding work that is in closer proximity to your home.

8. *Be aware of nature.* An instant way to take your stress level down a notch is to notice the natural beauty surrounding you. Make it a habit to notice three things in nature each time you drive—a cloud, a bird's song, a pretty sunrise or sunset, or a beautiful lake. If your commute takes you through urban or country roads, roll down your window or open your sunroof, and enjoy the fresh air.

9. *Be positive.* Negative thoughts create much of the stress in our lives. Search out and destroy any "awfulizing" or "what if" thoughts. Picture a big red "X" over the negative thought, or scream to yourself, "Cancel that thought!" Replace it with a positive image of enjoying success at work. Psych yourself up for a super day!

10. *Find a schedule-friendly sitter.* Your sitter may provide the world's greatest child care, but she's not worth it if her iron-clad "pick your child up by 6:00 P.M. or else" policy is stressing you out. Many parents drive at breakneck speeds to retrieve their children from child-care centers with inflexible schedules. Check out alternatives, such as a babysitter that is closer to your office, or one that has more leeway in her hours. This one change can free you from a major source of commuting stress.

POINTS TO REMEMBER

🙐 Your work life becomes more meaningful as you look for ways to give happiness and love in ordinary circumstances.

🙐 Guilt over money is a primary reason for financial problems. It's not "wrong" to want money, just to fret over the lack of it. Have faith, and you will always be supplied.

🙐 More and more people are hearing "the call" to become a professional healer. There are dozens of options open for training in traditional or alternative healing.

🙐 Commuting is a major source of energy-draining stress, which can impair productivity and concentration at work. However, steps such as planning ahead, ride-sharing, and making your car into a cocoonlike environment, reduce commuting stress.

🙐 🙐 🙐

Spiritual
Support

INTUITION AND YOUR INNER GUIDE

"If you knew Who walks beside you on the way that you have chosen, fear would be impossible."

— *A Course in Miracles*

W hat would you do if you suddenly discovered a no-cost source that you could turn to for:

+ Great ideas about how to solve any problem, make more money, and contribute to the world?
+ Complete emotional support, solace, and unconditional love?
+ One-hundred percent accurate predictions about the future?
+ Advice on any matter?

If you're like me, you'd stick to this source like glue. Well, there *is* such a source inside you right now, available to you day or night. Everyone has access to this source, regardless of his or her history. Just ask for its help, and you'll always receive it.

That source is your inner spiritual guide. As I've discussed throughout this book, your inner guide will guide you through every bit of completing your goals and fulfilling your divine assignment. It is your direct line to God, your way of phoning home and getting advice, consolation, and encouragement. All you need to do is become better acquainted with this invaluable resource in order to access its guidance, love, and support. Your inner guide wants to help you succeed, be happier, and be more prosperous. All you need to do is ask and listen.

The Best Help Around

Each of us has inner guides and angels who want to have more direct communication with us. At one time, I feared talking about this topic publicly. I was certain I would be scorned or mocked. As a fourth-generation metaphysician, I grew up in a household where God, Jesus, and angels were regular topics of discussion. I witnessed miracle healings and had spiritual encounters throughout my life. For example, my grandfather appeared at the foot of my bed one hour after he'd been killed by a drunk driver and told me he was at peace, and not to grieve.

However, growing up, my brother and I were cautioned against discussing these healings with anyone. We were told that spiritual healing was considered "kooky," so we just kept it to ourselves. As an adult, I continued to keep my spiritual knowledge under wraps, mostly out of habit and leftover fears. Today, though, spirituality is wide out in the open! Thanks to pioneering work by Louise Hay, Wayne Dyer, Marianne Williamson, Betty Eadie, Dr. Brian Weiss, Deepak Chopra, and others, at last we can freely discuss spiritual concepts.

Ever since I have begun talking more openly about my spiritual practices, none of my fears about ridicule have materialized. In fact, quite the opposite has occurred. Now that the word is spreading about my spiritual psychological work, requests from people who want to see me for counseling have gone up 200 percent.

So, I have overcome my fears about talking about the spiritual powers available to help us all. There is *so much more* that I'm excited to discuss with you in subsequent books about the lessons I've learned from my inner guide—wonderful lessons about heaven, eternal life, Jesus, and God. I'll share those in my future books and lectures, because they exceed the scope of this book for now.

Communicating with Your Inner Guide

We all have inner guides who can help us in any matter that is before us. These guides are like air traffic controllers: they have a bird's-eye view of what's in front, behind, and to each side of us. You have already experienced examples of their help if you've ever had a "voice" whisper advice to you, or had a force intervene in a near-accident. Our guides would like to help us even more often in our everyday activities, as well as our long-range plans. We just have to be open to their help.

My inner guide has given me great advice about career and finances, given me directions when I've been lost, told me the exact time I will arrive at my destination, given me prior warning and protection during an attempted car-jacking, offered reassurance about my brother's new business venture, and provided parenting tips and health and beauty advice.

Apparently, no subject is out of reach for our inner guides. One day, for example, I needed an outfit to wear to an important meeting. I turned the matter over to my guide, and was directed to a certain dress shop. Like a personal shopper, my inner guide steered me toward the perfect outfit at a great price, and my shopping was completed in under 30 minutes.

So many clients and readers have asked me for guidance on ways to hear the answers within. Many spiritual and self-help books advise "becoming still and hearing the still, small voice deep within oneself." Yet, my clients express frustration because they say that they can't hear anything. They feel like they're doing something wrong or wonder if their "communication line" is disconnected (or was never installed in the first place). Some of my clients, who suffer from shame connected to child abuse, wonder whether they missed out on being "issued" a inner guide or whether they didn't deserve one.

You, like everyone else, have lovingly been assigned a guide. No accidents or mistakes are possible in our orderly universe, and you do have one or more loving guides with you constantly. Guaranteed!

When I give my clients the information you're about to read, they are able to readily access this spiritual wisdom. Often, they are surprised to discover that the voice of the inner guide sounds similar to their own. Some people never hear a voice, however, because their lines of spirit communication aren't auditory.

We have four means of communication: visual (eyes), auditory (ears), kinesthetic (touch, smell, taste), and intuitive (hunches, gut feelings, or knowingness). Most people have one means of communication that they are strongest in, followed by a second strongest, and so forth.

When you receive communication from your inner guide (which you always will), it may not come as a voice or sound. So don't feel frustrated or like you're "flunking meditation" if you can't hear a still, small voice within. You must be more visual, kinesthetic, or intuitive instead of auditory. Sometimes, Spirit will give you a meaningful symbol, like showing you a mental image of a trophy to signal a coming victory, or the scent of a friend's cologne to signal you about that person's impending visit.

Linking Up

I help my clients get acquainted with their inner guides and offer them advice on how to communicate with them. Here are the steps we use for direct spirit links:

1. Practice daily meditation, and chakra cleansing and balancing, as explained in the next chapter. A healthful diet, avoiding negativity, and consistent exercise keep the "communication lines" open that connect you with Spirit.

2. Go within, and ask to speak with your inner guide.
3. Your communication link can be visual, auditory, intuitive, kinesthetic, or all four. Some people see their inner guides (in their mind's eye, or with eyes open); other people hear the voice of spirit's guidance (as a voice inside the head, or outside and separate); other people receive hunches or intuitions; and still others get guidance via smell, taste, and touch.

Hold a question in mind and then be ready for an answer (either through your sight, sound, intuition, or senses). You *will* be answered, that is for certain. What's not certain is whether you will trust the response. Many people, in the beginning, tend to discount spirit communication and think they've just imagined it.

If you don't understand or didn't quite hear your inner guide's answers, ask for clarification. Don't worry; your guide isn't going to be offended or run away! Just say to your inner guide, "A little louder, please," or "Could you show me that picture again, and let me know its meaning?" Of course, always say "Thank you" after you've received a communication.

As with anything, the more you practice, the easier it becomes to communicate with your inner guides. With patience and trust, you'll receive a lot of wonderful and important information. For me, inner guidance is like that credit card commercial: I won't leave home without it!

The Question of Surrender

Any person who has read about spirituality, recovery, or religion has encountered the word *surrender.* It means to let go of agendas and judgments about what life "should" look like or be like, and to instead accept life on life's terms. Surrender also means asking for help from a spiritual higher power, and not making decisions without first consulting this source.

The practice of surrendering everything to Spirit does create positive outcomes for several reasons:

+ There are very real and powerful spiritual forces that can intervene when we ask for help. The Law of Free Will means that our inner guides cannot help us unless we specifically ask for assistance (expect in the case of a life-threatening situation, where they do intervene even when we don't ask).

+ Surrendering makes us relax, and thus allows us to better hear our intuition. We find that we can get honest with ourselves about what we really believe and want, and then follow this inner wisdom. A relaxed state also allows creative solutions to bubble up from the subconscious, and into conscious awareness.

+ Surrendering triggers an ideal emotional state for creating cooperative relationships. Your faith and hope in trusting spiritual intervention makes for a loving and appealing personality that attracts other people. Studies show that the most attractive personality style, to men and women alike, is a warm, relaxed, and confident persona.

Managing Your Coincidences

Dr. Wayne Dyer coined the phrase, "Managing your coincidences," and by this phrase he means creating serendipitous situations that help you in reaching your ultimate goals and destinations.

Your intentions set the wheels of motion into action. Just by focusing on a question or a desire, you attract answers and help into your life. However, you must be alert to, and aware of, these solutions or you will miss seeing them. Many missed opportunities can be chalked up to a lack of awareness.

In the morning during your meditation, decide on a question or desire you'd like help with during the day. Then, hold on to the thought until you feel a sense of warm, happy peacefulness in your gut. This sensation is the feeling of faith; it's the magic glue that sets coincidences into motion. Know that you absolutely cannot fail in this endeavor, and that it works 100 percent of the time, provided you are aware and alert to the help when it knocks on your door.

But let's say that you hold a busy, time-consuming job during the day. Can you still manage your coincidences and create miracles that will help you in reaching your ultimate goals? Yes, of course you can!

As I was researching this book, I experienced a wonderful example of managing my coincidences. I posed the question: Why is there a pyramid and third eye or God-eye on the back of a dollar bill? I held this question in my mind, and knew that I would receive help and guidance (although, I must admit that I thought I'd be more apt to get my answer from a library book).

One Saturday, I thought about this question and promised myself that I'd go to the library the following week to find the answer. The following day, I flew to Las Vegas to autograph books at a convention. I climbed into a taxi at the airport and—with no prompting on my part—the taxi driver showed me a book he was reading about Free Masonry. Always interested in spirituality and religions, we engaged in a spirited discussion about church and state.

Suddenly, he pulled a dollar bill out of his wallet. "Strange," I thought, but said nothing. Imagine my delight and surprise when the cab driver pointed to the pyramid and God-eye on the back of the bill and began explaining the Free Masonry perspective on the history of these symbols!

Your God-Given Desires

Our deepest desires are no accident. They are imbedded deep within our hearts and minds, perhaps biologically programmed into us in the same way as genetic coding. Some spiritual theorists, including me, believe that we chose our purpose before entering the body at birth. Before entering into a body, we mapped out a life plan that would serve several purposes: the opportunity to balance karma from previous lives; the opportunity to perform selfless service for humanity; the opportunity to test our spiritual mettle by resisting material fears, temptations, and obsessions; the opportunity to completely let go and trust God's direction as given through our intuition; and the opportunity to discover that we are wholly perfect, whole, and complete.

So we created our divine assignments before we were born, and we remember and fulfill them through listening to and following our desires and intuition. It's almost like we have two missions here on earth: one is the physical form our function takes on (such as being a healer, a teacher, an artist, or whatever). The other mission is the underlying assignment given to every soul: to teach, give, and receive love.

While we're here on Earth, it's easy to get pulled away from the divine assignment either because we forget about it, or because we don't trust our intuition. If you forget or ignore your divine assignment, your intuition will nag at you incessantly. You'll feel anxious or depressed. You'll feel like you're forgetting to do something important (which you are). Some people try to turn off the intuition's nagging by taking medication, by overeating, drinking alcohol, impulsive spending, or some other compulsive activity. As you may have discovered firsthand, nothing can drown out the voice of your gut feelings. Nothing. The only reasonable choice is to follow your intuition, and discover how much joy and prosperity results from this choice.

If we don't fulfill our divine assignment while on Earth, we have ample opportunity to review our fears and mistakes during our after-death life review. You can elect to come back for another lifetime to have another go at it. A good book to read about this topic is *A World Beyond* by Ruth Montgomery.

Everyone has different divine assignments, dreams, and hopes. Your aspirations are uniquely yours (even though they may share some common elements with other people). Here is the question I'd like you to consider:

Where did your desires come from? I'm not talking about recent desires that may have been triggered by watching a television commercial or by seeing someone else's lifestyle. I'm talking about long-term desires, such as the yearnings you had as a little kid. For example, I've always wanted to be a published author. I used to write short stories for fun when I was very young, and submitted my first magazine article at age 14. I believe that I elected to become a self-help book author before I was born.

There is a definite flow of positive activity that occurs when we are on the right path. It's true that when you perform activities that give you great pleasure and that provide a useful function in the world, you will experience positive coincidences and support from others. You *will* find parking spaces easily. You *will* get appointments with people who can help you. You *will* get offers of assistance, money, and support as if by magic. And I believe this positive flow is the force called God; so in that respect, fulfilling your desires is the will of God.

You deserve a life that sails along smoothly. Embrace it. It's yours.

POINTS TO REMEMBER

🐸 We all have awesome spiritual support available to us, if only we will simply choose to ask for it.

🐸 All of us have inner guides to assist us in solving any problem in any area of our lives.

🐸 Our mental attitudes of positive expectations and surrender increase the amount of miracles in our lives.

SEE YOUR FUTURE, NOW!

"No man that does not see visions will ever realize any high hope or undertake any high enterprise."
—WOODROW WILSON (1856–1924),
28TH U.S. PRESIDENT/AUTHOR

N ow that you've set your goals, confronted any fears, and eased your schedule, it's time to coax your dreams into reality. Visualization is the best way to transform a wish into a living, breathing thing. Perhaps you've heard of visualization before, and maybe you've tried it.

My mother taught me to visualize when I was a small child, so the practice is second nature to me. I have used visualization to become published, to buy houses and cars, to lose weight, to receive more money, to take great vacations, to attract wonderful friends, and to find my love and soulmate, Michael.

Consistent Success

Many people who have read or heard about my successes with visualization have asked my advice on ways to use the method for more consistent successes. I always refer them to the best answer I have ever read, which was written by Emmet Fox in his wonderful pamphlet, *The Mental Equivalent*:

Many people fail to concentrate successfully because they think that concentration means will power. They actually try to concentrate with their muscles and blood vessels. They frown. They clench their hands. Unwittingly they are thinking of an engineer's drill or a carpenter's bit and brace. They suppose that the harder you press, the faster you get through. But all this is quite wrong.

Forget the drill and think of a camera. In a camera there is, of course, no question of pressure. There the secret lies in focus. If you want to photograph something, you focus your camera lens quietly, steadily, and persistently on the subject for the necessary length of time. Suppose I want to photograph a vase of flowers. What do I do? Well, I do not press it violently against the lens of the camera. That would be silly. I place the vase in front of the camera and keep it there. But suppose that after a few moments I snatch away the vase and hold a book in front of the camera, and then snatch that away and hold up a chair, and then put the flowers back for a few moments, and so forth. You know what will happen to my photograph. It will be a crazy blur. Is that not what people do to their minds when they cannot concentrate their thoughts for any length of time? They think health for a few minutes, and then they think sickness or fear. They think prosperity, and then they think depression. They think about bodily perfection, and then they think about old age and their pains and aches. Is it any wonder that we are apt to demonstrate the "marred image"?

Note carefully that I did not advocate taking one thought and trying to hold it through will power. You must allow a train of relevant thoughts to have free play in your mind, one leading naturally to the next, but they all must be positive, constructive, harmonious, and pertain to your desire; and you must think quietly and without effort.

A Brief History of Visualization

We tend to think of "visualization"—the act of controlling thoughts and mental images to create positive life changes—as a product of modern times. Surprisingly, though, the practice has a very ancient and holy history. The use of visualization and imagery appears to be as old as human beings themselves, and to be a part of many ancient and modern religions.

Descriptions of humans' use of visualization go back as far as 60,000 B.C.! During the Ice Age, hunters painted pictures of their animal prey on cave walls. Archeologists believe that the hunters threw spears at these animal paintings as a way of visualizing a successful hunt. This isn't much different than modern-day Olympic athletes' use of precompetition visualization.

Almost every ancient culture shows evidence of the use of visualization as a tool in healing and worship. Ancient Egyptian philosophy stated that everything in the universe was based on mind, not matter. Further, the Egyptians believed that thoughts have powerful energy vibrations that change and control matter. The Egyptians taught that "transmutation" (which they later called "alchemy")—the process of focusing and controlling one's thoughts—could transform emotions of fear into feelings of love. They also believed that if we hold a sacred thought in mind, we could heal ourselves and everyone else in the world through the power of our highly attuned thought energy. The Egyptians used visualization for physical healings, as well. They believed that disease was cured by visualizing perfect health and by holding this image in mind.

Greek cultural philosophies about healing with visualization appear to have been influenced by the Egyptians. Greek healers often prescribed a sort of "dream therapy" for their patients, asking them to induce dreams of being healed by gods.

Visualization in the form of focused thought and concentration was a key part of the Yoga Sutra lifestyle in 200 B.C. The Yoga Sutras taught that by holding a single image in mind, one could bliss-fully connect with the truth of that image. Tantric Yoga, developed in sixth century A.D., taught that humans' labels and judgments blocked them from knowing the truth about themselves and life. To counteract this negative tendency, Tantrists developed a method of consciously visualizing a divine image. The goal was to experience a union with the divine image and to free the flow of energy throughout the body. Tantric visualization also involved staring at a geometrical shape, called a "mandala," until you felt at one with the image. This was a means of centering oneself with visualization.

The Bible contains many references to belief and faith as keys to creating changes in life. One of the more profound promises made by Jesus is in Matthew 21:22: "And all things, whatsoever ye shall ask in prayer, believing, ye shall receive." This point is made again in Mark 9:23: "…all things are possible to him that believeth."

Indian healers, medicine men and women, and shamans have used visualization as a means of healing. Shamans believe that ill-ness is triggered by a disconnection with one's soul. So, they vi-sualize finding and retrieving the ill person's soul, and reuniting him or her as a whole being. Navaho Indians use group visualiza-tions to heal illness. These organized efforts involve group mem-bers seeing the ill person as perfectly healed and healthy.

Renowned 16th-century physician Paracelsus stated that, "The power of the imagination is a great factor in medicine. It may pro-duce diseases in man and it may cure them." In 1604, Thomas Wright wrote that visualization healed through the process of "spirits" that "flock from the brain, by certain secret channels to the heart."

Visualization has been around for many, many years. Its popu-larity was revived in the late 1800s and early 1900s by authors, spiritual healers, and religious leaders such as Napoleon Hill, Claude M. Bristol, Ralph Waldo Emerson, Ernest Holmes (Reli-gious Science), and Mary Baker Eddy (Christian Science).

In the early 1980s, Louise L. Hay took visualization and her self-published book, *You Can Heal Your Life*, from its mimeographed origins to the *New York Times* bestseller list. In Norman Cousins' landmark book, *Anatomy of an Illness,* he wrote about increasing the white blood cell count by visualizing them as white cowboys lassoing diseased tissue. The 1980s also saw visualization popularized as a tool for enhancing career, financial, and material success. Today, the U.S. Olympic Committee advocates using visualization to enhance performance in all athletic pursuits. Harvard researchers are investigating the links between visualization and the immune system.

My prediction is that, in the next decade, virtual reality machines will trigger an explosion of interest in visualization. More and more people will see how reliable a method it is for manifestation. These machines will be used to "test drive" different futures for yourself. Once you find one that you like, you will visualize it until it manifests into reality. At that point, visualization will become as widely accepted a practice as it was in prehistoric times.

Specify Everything

Visualization always works, and it works so well that you must be very careful to specify exactly what you want. Since I've used visualization my entire life, I'm able to almost instantly manifest anything. Sometimes I'll ask for something and then become startled by how quickly I receive it.

For example, I decided that the house I lived in was too small, especially now that my sons have grown into six-foot giants. So, I visualized (in splendid detail) moving to a different home. That afternoon, a Realtor called because someone inquired about buying my house. *"Wait a moment,"* I thought. *"This is too fast! I'm not sure I really want to move from this house."* So, I mentally 'X'd' out the image, and the real estate deal fell through as a result.

Then, every time I'd visualize my "new" house, a Realtor would call me. Finally, I became honest with myself and admitted I didn't want to move from my present location. The boys will be out of the house attending college soon, anyway, I decided.

Another experience that helped me realize the importance of being specific during visualization was in my love life. You may recall me describing my lukewarm results in manifesting John, the rose-bearing C.P.A. I had affirmed my desire for a boyfriend who gave me roses, without adding other, more vital details to my wish list. Well, I'd forgotten one small but important detail. I forgot to specify that he would be a man I would be attracted to. The truth was that my feelings for John were about as flat as if he'd been my kid brother. Was I ever sorry about that, believe me!

So, the next time, I put a few more details on my visualization "love request." I asked for a romantic man who wanted to get married and who I would have an intense attraction toward. Boom! Again, the universe delivered to my exact specifications. This time, I received a French-Canadian man who would sing me love songs, buy me gifts, and who asked me to marry him one month after we'd met. I was extremely attracted to him, but again I found that I'd left off important details in my visualization—details that would preclude me from marrying him.

Well, the third time was a charm. This time, I decided to go for broke and specify every single detail I could think of that was important to me in a husband. I put down everything: his temperament, health practices, type of employment, where he lived, political affiliation, hair color, eye color—the whole bit. Some people have asked me whether such a complete and detailed list is limiting. I'm here to tell you that it's the opposite: it frees you to meet the man or woman of your dreams!

After I wrote that list, I completed the next most vital step in visualization. I turned the matter over in perfect faith to God. I absolutely knew that this man of my dreams was looking for me just as earnestly as I was looking for him. And every time I would close my eyes while knowing this truth, an image of a white kitchen countertop overlooking a body of water would enter my mind.

One week after I made my list, my inner guide strongly directed me to do some things that eventually led me to walk into a small French restaurant near my home. In the entryway, I bumped into a tall man with smiling blue eyes. It was incredible; I actually recognized him as the man I had envisioned. We sat down and talked, and every single thing I'd written down was part of this man's life and character. Michael and I have been together ever since that day, and my love life is a real-life dream come true. (By the way, when I walked into his house for the first time, I wasn't surprised to see the white kitchen countertop overlooking Newport Beach harbor, just as I'd seen it in my mind's eye. There are no coincidences!)

You can use visualization to attract anything you want, and to heal any situation in your life. For example, in Chapter 11, I discuss how my clients and I use visualization to heal soured marriages, parental problems, and other family rifts.

Visualization is easier if you hang pictures representing your desires and look at them often. When I wanted a Hawaiian vacation, for instance, I hung photos of palm trees and white sandy beaches and pictured myself basking in the tropical sunshine. That visualization prompted my family to save for a summertime two-week trip to the big island of Hawaii. I've cut out pictures that helped me get a new car, lose weight, and get published at particular book publishing companies.

Whatever you want is yours, if you will only allow yourself to see it and know it.

Self-Improvement Is Natural

The desire to improve one's life is a natural, innate one. We enter a body and live on this planet for the express purpose of soul growth. In life and after death, we continually evolve into more loving, honest, and forthright souls. It's impossible to remove the desire for positive movement and self-improvement from our beings. It's built in!

You have powerful spiritual help available to you right now. Perhaps you're aware of this because you've felt a presence or force during meditation or a near-accident. Perhaps you think such an idea is impractical and silly. Whatever your position about spiritual help from God, angels, and inner guidance, you probably wouldn't turn down divine intervention or a miracle if it were offered to you.

You are not alone, and have never been alone. God has always met, and will always meet, your every human need. If you think back over the years, you'll see that He always took care of you and that you never starved or became completely destitute. He won't let you down now or ever, and if you faithfully depend upon His assistance, the help will keep increasing. Let go of your fears and concerns about your body, and focus instead on fulfilling your divine assignment.

God, the infinite creator, made us in His image and likeness. Consequently, we too are natural creators. We have incessant desires to create, and we have the power to manifest these creations. A Creator created us.

The greatest spiritual works affirm that God wants us to enjoy a rich and abundant life and that prosperity is a natural result of right thinking and right action:

+ From *The Bible*: "Beloved, I wish above all things that thou mayest prosper."

+ From *Anguttara Nikaya* (Buddhism): "At the thought, 'By means of wealth acquired...I both enjoy my wealth and do meritorious deeds,' bliss comes to him, satisfaction comes to him. This is called 'the bliss of wealth.'"

+ From *A Course in Miracles*: "God is not willing that His Son be content with less than everything."

+ From *Yoruba Proverbs* (African Traditional Religion): "There is no place where one cannot achieve greatness; only the lazy prospers nowhere."

+ From *The Avesta* (Zoroastrianism, India) : "Let one practice here good industry; let one make the needy prosperous."
+ From *The Koran* (Islam): "When the prayer is finished, scatter in the land and seek God's bounty, and remember God frequently, that you may prosper."
+ From *Great Learning* (Confucianism): "Virtue is the root; wealth is the result."

Almost without exception, world religions emphasize that material comfort becomes a detriment to soul growth only if one focuses on it instead of focusing on God. However, if we work and interact lovingly, spiritual law automatically fulfills our material needs. We need only remember love, and have faith in our Source, and His effects (prosperity) are natural. It is only when we focus on the effects and forget our Source, that we experience fear, guilt, anger, insecurity, and financial ills.

God's Will

"What if what I want isn't God's will for me?" Many of my clients feel confused and stuck by this question.

My answer is based upon my lifelong study and experiences dealing with this question. Here's a synopsis of my spiritual background, so you'll understand the foundation for my beliefs. I was conceived, born, and raised in a very spiritual household. My mother, a third-generation metaphysician and spiritual healer, and my father, an author of inspirational books, had tried unsuccessfully to conceive a baby for many years. My mother submitted a prayer request to a Religious Science prayer ministry, and less than a month later, she was pregnant with me.

My family was devoted to studying spiritual truths in the metaphysical churches, Unity, Religious Science, and Christian Science. Since my mother was a spiritual healer, miracles were a natural occurrence for me as I grew up. So, I've never known anything different from metaphysical principles such as affirming, visualizing, healing, and manifesting one's greatest good.

However, nothing had prepared me for what happened to me when I was eight years old as I walked out of the Unity Church one Sunday afternoon. Something made me stop. The scene around me shifted, and I felt a forceful pressure simultaneously outside and inside me. Suddenly, I saw myself from a vantage point about one foot to the right of where my body was, as if my spirit was outside my body. It all happened so fast!

Then, a male voice communicated to me through a combination of auditory words, palpable vibrations, and an intuitive knowingness. The voice explained that I was experiencing an example of the split between mind and body. It explained that the spirit or the mind was the only thing real, and that the body was at the command of the mind. He then told me, "You are here to teach people that the mind controls the body."

Then, just as quickly, the voice went away and my normal vision returned. Although it was definitely an out-of-the-ordinary occurrence, I felt safe and accepting. I had just been helped to remember my Divine Purpose.

After that day, the power of this divine assignment became more and more evident. Whenever I neglected my purpose, it would gnaw away at me and not let me rest. In my early 20s, I tried to ignore the mission and grew unhappy, overweight, and restless. I had no choice but to accept and fulfill my purpose, so I became a spiritually based psychotherapist and self-help author. All the doors opened the moment I made that commitment.

Today, I immediately realize when I stray away from my Divine Purpose. For example, I've tried a few times to write books about topics that were "off my path" and always met with total failure. I couldn't even make one penny! I was always stressed, voraciously hungry, or just generally unhappy every time I attempted to veer off my path.

I realize that most people don't hear a heavenly voice that directs them on their career paths. I don't know why God so clearly gave the assignment to me, but He did. I've found, though, that I can easily help others find *their* Divine Purpose. Within a few minutes of meeting someone, I readily sense which career paths would best suit and fulfill this person.

Your Divine Purpose

My beliefs and opinions about divine assignments, purpose, goals, and missions stem from a devout study encompassing almost 40 years. I firmly believe the following:

First, I think that God gives us our long-lasting desires. In other words, our tastes and enjoyment for certain activities and lifestyles are as God-given as our hair and eye color. He doesn't will suffering, and He wants to meet our material needs so we can fulfill our function of happiness and soul growth. Food, shelter, and money concerns distract us off our spiritual paths. So, fulfilling your material needs leaves your mind and soul free to concentrate on higher aspirations.

The Bible and other great spiritual works of the world direct us to have faith that God will meet our material needs as long as we are following our divine path. We ask for what we want, believe God will give it, and we receive it. Worrying slows receipt of the good that we deserve and need because it makes us feel separate from our Source instead of surrendering into His loving care. Worrying about how we'll pay tomorrow's bills also creates an obsessive focus on material gain, which takes our focus off the faith that God supplies all our needs.

We mustn't wonder or worry *how* our needs will be supplied. The *how* is up to God, not us. Trying to direct how we will fulfill goals is called "outlining," a violation of spiritual law and a guaranteed way not to get your desires. Our focus needs to stay on what we want, on being grateful for, and trusting of, God's power.

Your success is "spiritually correct" because it inspires others to fulfill their highest functions. Think about the writers, authors, and speakers you most admire, and ask yourself whether you would still follow their philosophies if they were living on welfare or in a homeless shelter. We put more stock in the ideologies of people who take good care of themselves. Even the Bible says, "The poor man's wisdom is despised, and his words are not heard."

What about knowing which career path is our divine purpose? I believe that we all have a God-given purpose on this earth. Our primary purpose is loving and forgiving ourselves and others. We also have careers that are divinely directed. There are two parts to your career path. The first is always to maintain peace of mind and act in loving ways no matter what job you hold.

The second is to enter a career that dovetails with your purpose for being here. Your career purpose always involves some function that serves and helps the world. This could involve teaching, entertaining, enlightening, consulting, counseling, or helping others to run their businesses or home more smoothly.

Your divinely appointed career involves your natural talents and interests. Some people doubt that work can be enjoyable. It can! Being in your right career is a blast! Because the work is enjoyable, we put more time and effort into it, and we naturally prosper ourselves and the world.

The world lets you know when you're on the right path. Doors open wide and abundantly offer opportunities. Money comes to you, and people offer to help. Yes, you do have to exert effort, but it flows naturally!

What You Think About Always Comes About

As a result of my metaphysical upbringing, which told me as a child that there are no limits, I have always been able to see things such as energy fields and inner guides. When I talk to anyone, whether in person or on the phone, I see images and pictures of their family members, their hobbies, or their goals. Some people refer to this as a "psychic" ability. I prefer to think of it as a normal skill that we all possess, but that many choose to turn off or ignore.

What you think about, especially when thoughts are combined with strong emotions, is carved out in your energy field (the essence around you that is sometimes called your *aura*). If you think about an object, people like me who are sensitive to energy fields can actually see that object as if it is floating next to you. It's a little like looking at glowing white cookie dough that has had a cookie cutter stamped out of it in full 3-D detail.

A psychic isn't so much predicting your future, but is more often seeing images in your aura that you have projected there through your thought patterns. If you are thinking a lot about getting a sports car, there will be energy equivalent to a sports car in your field. Eventually, if you hold that thought long enough, that energy equivalent will manifest into the real thing, and you'll be holding the steering wheel of a sports car. Now, a psychic can see that energy image and will tell you something such as, "I see you driving a sports car."

Wowwee! you'll think, that's the future I want! You'll gladly pay the psychic his or her $40 or $50 fee, but what you must know is that the prediction will only come true if you continue to think about that sports car. If you change your mental image to, for example, thoughts that "I can't afford a new car," then you have instantly altered your future.

Your thoughts are powerful magnets and messengers. Guard your thoughts, and only choose images that match what you want in your life. In that way, you will only attract experiences, people, and things that you truly desire.

Outlining Versus Designing

Visualize the end result that you want—the financial, love, health, or career situation that would blend with your ideals. But don't, I repeat, don't specify how you are going to get the desired result. The "what" of your desires is up to you; the "how" you're going to get it is completely up to God.

If you try and outline a plan of manifestation in your visualizations, you will block the ingenious plans that your inner guides have for you. Let's say you visualize having a wonderful job in your chosen field making a $100,000-a-year salary. That is your "what" in visualization, and by deciding what you want, you have fulfilled your end of the bargain.

The "how," though, needs to be released.

Let's say you go on a job interview and it seems like the exact job you've been hoping for. So you go home and visualize the interviewer calling you up and offering you the job. You have just outlined the how, and that is in violation of spiritual law. Your visualization will probably come true, and the interviewer will offer you the job just as you imagined.

But what if that wasn't the best job for you? What if the next job interview would have been for an even better job with more opportunities, benefits, and a higher salary? You have missed that divine opportunity by insisting the universe give you the first job. That's why it's important to specifically decide what you want, but to surrender the means by which you'll get it.

Another example is when a person is visualizing getting a material object, such as a new house. It's a great idea to visualize what kind of house you want and its general geographical location. Even go into what kind of neighbors you want, and any other details that appeal to you. Just don't tell the universe which exact house you want, or worry about how to pay for it.

When you surrender the "how," you free your inner guides and angels to creatively finance your desired objective. Many people who have set their sights on a new house, car, vacation, or wardrobe were pleasantly surprised by how the money just "appeared" from some unexpected source. I, and several others I know, have even gotten houses for no money down by using visualization.

Remember, there are no limits to what you can be, have, or do...unless you decide that there are limits. I hope you've decided to become a limitless person, free to experience and enjoy all the delicacies that life has to offer!

The Power of Affirmations

We call positive thoughts worded in present-tense terms "affirmations." Most likely, you have used affirmations—perhaps without realizing it! Telling yourself something like, "I'm a winner!" is an example of an affirmation.

I have used affirmations for dramatic and rapid transformation in my personal and professional life. As I have written about previously, affirmations helped me to fulfill my desires. You may recall me telling you that at one time, I was a fat, unhappy, and uneducated housewife. My inner guide kept pushing me to get a psychology degree and write books, but inside I wondered if I would fail. Affirmations helped me to know that I could do it and that I deserved success.

Here are some affirmations designed to reduce and eliminate fear or anxiety. If any of these phrases strike a chord with you, write them down, and post them in a conspicuous location, such as on your bathroom mirror, in your wallet, or on your car dashboard. I also recommend listening to an affirmation tape or CD, either one that you make yourself or one professionally made (such as those available through my publisher, Hay House).

AFFIRMATIONS FOR SELF-CONFIDENCE

+ I am safe and secure.

+ I trust my intuition to guide me.

+ I have enough time, money, and intelligence to accomplish my goals.

+ I know that I am guided toward good today.

+ I deserve all that is good.

+ When I win, others win as well.

+ I always find time to fulfill my dreams.

+ I am blessed in many ways.

+ Other people like and respect me.

+ My efforts are always supported and encouraged.

+ God always takes care of my every human need.

+ I am devoted to teaching the world about love.

+ I take advantage of spare moments in the day, and my small efforts add up to large accomplishments.

+ My body obeys my every command.

+ Abundance is a safe and comfortable condition.

+ Today, my thoughts center on love and success.

+ I expect and experience a happy outcome in every situation.

+ I am relaxed, poised, and confident.

+ My peacefulness serves as a model and inspiration for others.

+ I am guilt free in all respects.

+ I naturally attract positive people and conditions.

+ Everything I accomplish builds my confidence even more.

+ I accept good graciously.

+ My voice is reassuring, both to myself and to others.

+ I have unlimited energy.

- God's Will for me is perfect happiness.
- Other people are happy about my goals and accomplishments.
- I give myself permission to change my life.
- I expect and receive peaceful cooperation from others.
- My faith and beliefs are unwavering.
- I take action to fulfill my Divine Purpose.
- I am inspired and I am creative.
- My investment of meditation time pays huge dividends.
- My wisdom guides me to use time for the highest and best good of everyone.
- Other people respect my needs and wishes.
- I attract loving, successful people into my life.
- I enjoy taking steps toward the accomplishment of my goals.
- I boldly trust and obey the instructions of my inner wisdom.
- Today, I complete one or more steps that move me closer to my dream life.

POINTS TO REMEMBER

❧ You can use visualization to positively change your love, work, and health life.

❧ Humans have used visualization since primitive times. Today, professional athletes use visualization for increased performance, and medical researchers use visualization for rapid and miraculous healings.

❧ Decide what you want, affirm it, and then leave the "how" up to the universe.

WHERE ALL PROBLEMS ARE SOLVED, AND ALL QUESTIONS ARE ANSWERED

"Before embarking on important undertakings, sit quietly, calm your senses and thoughts and meditate deeply. You will then be guided by the great creative power of Spirit."

— PARAMAHANSA YOGANANDA

I've talked a lot about meditation in this book for one primary reasons: *it works so well in so many ways.* There is no "right" way to meditate and no set amount of time that is necessary (except that it's a good idea to meditate first thing in the morning and immediately before retiring for the night).

Some people with hectic schedules say they have no time for meditation. However, *A Course in Miracles* emphasizes that it's quality, not quantity, that counts in meditation. I agree, and believe that even one minute of focused meditation yields amazing benefits. I'd rather see someone commit to having a connection with their source for one minute than to sit with wandering or idle thoughts for one hour.

The time you devote to deep meditation will actually streamline your schedule! You'll feel alert and energized after meditation, and things won't irritate you as much. As a result, you'll have fewer time-consuming arguments with others. Studies show that meditation lowers blood pressure, and that people who meditate visit doctors less frequently. All facets of life—in addition to one's schedule—improve with meditation.

The Bliss of Meditation

So many spiritual leaders have emphatically endorsed meditation as a means to receive answers, comfort, and enlightenment! From Paramahansa Yogananda: *"The greatest love you can experience is in communion with God in meditation. The love between the soul and Spirit is the perfect love, the love you are all seeking. When you meditate, love grows. Millions of thrills pass through your heart...If you meditate deeply, a love will come over you such as no human tongue can describe; you will know His divine love, and you will be able to give that pure love to others."*

From the Bible: *"Do not neglect the gift that is in you, which was given to you by prophesy with the laying on of the hands of the eldership. Meditate on these things; give yourself entirely to them, that your progress may be evident to all."*

From *A Course in Miracles*: *"Try to remember when there was a time—perhaps a minute, maybe even less—when nothing came to interrupt your peace; when you were certain you were loved and safe. Then try to picture what it would be like to have that moment be extended to the end of time and to eternity. Then let the sense of quiet that you felt be multiplied a hundred times, and then be multiplied another hundred more. And now you have a hint, not more than just the faintest intimation of the state your mind will rest in when the truth has come. Without illusions there could be no fear, no doubt and no attack."*

One Meditation Method

I'll go over some brief guidelines for meditation, because so many people have asked me for them. Keep in mind that meditation has no goals; you can't do it right or wrong. It doesn't really matter how long you meditate; what's most important is the quality. By quality I mean that during your meditation you reach an emotional and physical response that we could describe as peace, as a warm feeling of love, as a falling into the arms of your spiritual and divine source.

Your life may dramatically transform in response to consistent meditation. While at first, you may worry about how much time needs to be involved, soon you will want to incorporate meditation into your life on a permanent basis. Meditation is an excellent stress-management tool. It's also a beauty secret; it actually erases lines of worry and tension and gives your complexion a rosy inner glow. It makes the eyes shine with youth and joy, and helps the spirit feel alive and energized.

Many people, myself included, wouldn't dream of missing meditation. I recommend that you meditate every single morning and evening. This doesn't have to take a lot of time; just ten minutes is enough. However, on those days when you can make more time, you certainly will find benefits to lengthier meditations.

One of those benefits is finding answers to your most important questions—questions concerning finances, which career path you would most enjoy and prosper at, questions about your love life, about your health, and even about other people. The answers almost magically come into consciousness during meditation. I've also had instances of guidance, of warnings about things that might happen during the day (and which did actually occur). Since I had meditated and heard these warnings, I was prepared. So, I have found that meditation is a great investment of my time.

Meditation means that you hold your focus on thoughts from your higher self, or no thoughts at all. This does take some power of concentration because, as it says in *A Course in Miracles*, the source of so many of our problems is that we are undisciplined in our minds. We allow our ego—which is the place within us that holds fear and guilt thoughts—to run rampant with our life, thoughts, and feelings. We are often victims of our own selves and our own thinking.

We can pull ourselves out of those ego-based thoughts of fear and guilt, which seem to control us, by knowing that we have control over the thoughts that we choose. If you are facing life challenges, you can best solve them by using your full faculties, which are borne of calm, clear thinking and do not harbor any fears.

Here are some ways to make meditation especially effective and enjoyable:

— Prepare a quiet, private place to retreat to in the morning soon after awakening, and in the evening before you retire. This place does not have to be very large. It could be a corner of a bedroom, or even a bathroom. The only thing that's important is that you will be uninterrupted during your meditation.

— Ask for the cooperation of the people you live with. Ask your family members or roommates to honor your time alone. Know that you are giving them the gift of your increased energy and positive moods, which are the beneficial results of meditation.

— Set a schedule and stick to it. At first, you may want to schedule your meditation in ink on your calendar so that you've made a firm promise to yourself. Make a commitment that, for at least seven days in row, no matter what comes up, you will meditate.

— Find a comfortable sitting position where your back is straight, perhaps supported by a wall or a cushion. Position your legs comfortably, but don't cross them (which would block your flow of energy). Sitting in a lotus position or with your legs in front of you is fine, whatever feels best to you.

— Close your eyes to block out all external distractions so that your inner vision can take over.

Here is a wonderful morning meditation to start your day off on a miraculous note:

MORNING MEDITATION

Begin by taking a deep breath. Draw in as much air as you possibly can through your nose. Breathe in and hold the breath, and then exhale slowly out of your mouth, blowing all of the air out of your lungs. Take another deep breath through your nose, holding in all of the air and all of the energy from this air, and then blowing out through your mouth all the air, and along with it all the cares, concerns, worries, or fears that may block you. Breathe in courage, love, gratitude, and excitement, and hold all these positive energies within you. Blow out anything that smacks of fear or guilt, knowing that these only interfere with fulfillment of your mission and purpose.

As you continue to breathe in and out very deeply, you may notice that you begin to feel more and more alive and energized. You are ready to take on the day and to fulfill your deepest aspirations and desires. Know that you are a gift to the world, to yourself, and to others when you are on your divine path. To get on this path, and stay on this path, it is so important for you to be centered and perfectly calm, and this meditation will help bring you back to center, to that place where all intelligence and all energy stems from.

You know that you are a divine being and that you do deserve all of the riches and all of the good of the universe. You do deserve to have your dreams come true. You are perfect! You are whole! You are complete! You are

*loved and loving, and you have so much to give. And the
way to give is by being completely unblocked, releasing
all fear, because fear is not of you—it is an illusion, and
we now surrender all fears and all worries and we go forward to feeling the strength and the power that is within.*

This meditation is useful for receiving answers and guidance:

MEDITATION TO CONTACT YOUR INNER GUIDE

*Bring your attention inward, and breathe deeply. See or
feel a straight line of lightning-white energy running
through the top of your head, down the center of your
body, and out through the floor. As you focus on this energy, notice your emotions and energy levels becoming
peaceful and harmonious.*

*At this time, you may want to access some information
from your inner guide. As you go inward to the place
where all answers are available to you, trust the information that you are given, and do not discount anything.
Some people receive answers to their questions in the
form of symbols or pictures. Other people hear a voice—
sometimes the voice sounds like their very own. Other
times, the voice sounds like that of someone else. Many
people receive their answers in the form of hunches or intuitive feelings—they just know the answer.*

*Whether you receive your answers through auditory, vi-
sual, or kinesthetic forms is unimportant. What is important is that you do ask for help, because the Law of
Free Will says that our guides cannot help us unless we
ask for help. It is also important that you trust, and deeply
consider heeding the information that you are given. Your
inner guide can give you information for anything, small
or large. Your inner guide can warn you if danger is about*

to come up, or tip you off if something is an opportunity for your career advancement. Turn everything over to this guide, and you will always be well ahead of the game.

So let us now turn inward, to the place where all intelligence resides. Focus your mind, and do not allow it to wander on to mundane or unimportant things, unless they specifically relate to your question. It's important to come up with a clear intention or question in your heart, for it is the words of your heart that your guides and the universe pay attention to. So make sure your question does come from the heart and is sincere, and go ahead and ask the question whenever you're ready, and then go in, in, in, sinking into the arms of your guide. Let yourself sink. Give yourself permission to let go.

Go inward, go inward. Sink down. Let go. Go inward. Focus and listen. Focus and listen. Listen to your inner guide. Focus, focus. And listen, knowing that you will always be answered. You will always receive the answer to every question. All you have to do is listen and trust. Go within. Feel alive, refreshed, and know that you can do it! You are competent! You are successful! You are free, and you can make changes and you will be safe as you make these changes.

You do deserve complete abundance in your life, and as you follow your heart and follow the guidance of your inner wisdom, you know that you will always be taken care of. You do not have to worry about time, money, or intelligence, because those very worries will cause problems and blocks in your life. So it is important that you do not allow yourself to worry, fret, or be concerned. All you need to do is to honor the important path and purpose that has been assigned to you, so accept this now. You do deserve to have a career that makes you happy, and a love life that is harmonious and filled with bliss. You do de-

serve to have radiant, perfect health and to have rela-
tionships that are balanced and harmonious.
Go inward, down. Down inward. Listen.

This is a powerful meditation for increasing your energy and intuition:

CLEANSING AND BALANCING YOUR CHAKRAS

Your powers are influenced by seven energy centers in
your body called "chakras." Each chakra performs a
unique task. I have found that the act of cleansing and
balancing these chakras is incredibly powerful and results
in heightened awareness and increased intuition, energy,
and confidence. So, let's begin by picturing your chakras,
and cleansing and balancing each one, so that today you
have access to everything that is within you—all of your
gifts, information, and power.

Start by picturing your "root chakra," at the base of
your spine. This is a ruby-red ball, perfect in every way.
Picture a bright, white light like a halogen spotlight,
glowing over that red ball, illuminating it from the inside.
This chakra, when balanced and cleansed by this white
light as you are doing right now, allows you to express
your individuality, your unique expression of creativity
and intelligence. It also helps you in maintaining har-
monious relationships with everyone you encounter
throughout the day.

Just as you are a perfect creation of the divine Creator,
so too are all the people you will encounter today. Even
though appearances may suggest that people are prac-
ticing loveless behavior, just concentrate on the truth deep
inside these other people. Know that they embody perfect
love and harmony. Through your unbending intent and

*focus on the truth, these other individuals will miracu-
lously treat you with consideration and cooperation.
Other people always respond to our expectations, so
today, with this balanced root chakra, release any fears
or judgments about others. Stay only in the present moment and expect only good behavior and treatment from
others—including yourself. And so it is!*

*Now move up to the second chakra, the sacral chakra,
located about three inches below your navel. See in this
sacral chakra a perfect orange light, round in its sphere.
Focus the same white light on this orange sphere until it
illuminates from the center with perfect orange beauty.
The sacral chakra is your center for desire, and as you
cleanse and balance this chakra with the white light, your
desires become balanced and harmonious.*

*You do deserve all of your desires to come true, and you
now embrace and accept your divine dreams. You do deserve good in your life, and complete abundance in all
areas of love, work, money, health, and everything else
that comes to you throughout the day. We all deserve
good, and it is God's good pleasure to give us the king-
dom of heaven here on earth. So we now balance our desires by no longer fearing or feeling guilty about what it
is that we truly want. We now graciously accept help from
others, and we graciously accept good coming into our
life now.*

*At this point, move up to the "solar plexus" chakra,
which is located behind the navel. Here you can see a perfect yellow light, a little sun, round and glowing. Shine the
white, bright spotlight on this yellow jewel and make it il-
luminate even further. The solar plexus chakra is the center of power and control.*

*As you balance and cleanse this area, see your desires
for power and control come into perfect harmony. You*

*have no fear of losing power or control. You never strug-
gle with others to try and regain what you could never
lose in the first place. Since you no longer struggle, other
people are inspired to help and cooperate. Feel the
warmth throughout the stomach region. Feel the warmth
that comes from your true power, the power given to you
by your Creator—the power that you can never lose and
that you can access at any moment.*

*Be grateful for this power, and as you tap into it, know
that you will use it throughout the day. This power and
this control are now used for your, and for others', highest and best good. And so it is!*

*Now move your attention up to the heart region,
where you see a beautiful emerald-green ball, a beautiful jewel that is the "heart chakra." Shine the white,
bright spotlight on this green ball and bathe yourself in
beautiful feelings of love for all of humanity. Allow the
love to permeate throughout your body until your fingers
begin to tingle and your breath becomes shallow and you
feel the delicious sensation of love. Love. Love for all, for
your life and for others.*

*Move up to the throat, to the "throat chakra," located
near your Adam's apple, where there is a light blue ball,
a beautiful sphere of light blue light. As you shine the
white spotlight on the throat chakra, see that it sparkles
with illuminated light blue. This is your center for communication, and you give thanks, because now that your
throat chakra is perfectly cleansed and balanced, you
know that throughout the day you will be able to express
yourself in verbal or written forms. We've now unblocked all communication, so you will easily express
yourself to others in all situations today.*

*Move up to the area between your two eyes, to the
"third eye" chakra. You can see a dark blue ball, inter-*

spersed with little flashes of white light and sometimes purple light. You can also see, if you look closely enough, a third eye looking back at you. This third eye is your center of intuition and inner vision. This is the center where you receive information that can keep you safe and make you successful. You can now shine the bright white spotlight on the third eye chakra, so that your inner vision is perfectly cleansed and perfectly balanced. You now have complete access to all of the wisdom of the universe. Release anything that could block your inner vision. Release all fears, all judgments, all resentments, all worries, and any sense of guilt or pressure. As you release these illusions from your consciousness, you'll find that the window of your inner vision is perfectly washed and cleansed and sparkling clear, like a new pair of glasses.

Now move up to the "crown chakra," which is located at the top of the head on the inside. This is a beautiful purple ball. The crown chakra is the place where spiritual wisdom from the universe enters into your consciousness. Shine the white light on this purple jewel, cleansing and balancing your crown chakra, so you have easy access to all information that you want or need. As you open up this crown chakra, you may picture a funnel, going in from the top of your head into your crown chakra and into your mind. Know that this crown chakra will allow the loving information of God and the universe to enter your mind easily throughout the day, so that you are never alone and so that you always have a guide with you.

Now take the white light and move it out through the crown chakra and surround your body entirely in the white light for perfect protection throughout the day. Then seal your entire body in green light for perfect health. Finally, surround yourself with the purple violet light of spirituality, so that now nothing but good can happen to you throughout the day. You are perfectly cleansed, balanced, and protected.

I recommend this meditation for cleansing your soul of any worries or upsets, so you can have a peaceful night's sleep:

EVENING MEDITATION

It's time to release any cares, concerns, worries, fears, or anything negative collected in your consciousness or body today. Just as you wash your face every evening before going to bed, it's important to also spiritually cleanse yourself before drifting off to sleep. This meditation is designed to give you high-quality sleep and to help you remember your dreams for continuing guidance and creative inspiration.

Sitting in your comfortable, upright meditation position, start with a deep breath where you drink in refreshing thoughts and feelings. When you're ready, deeply exhale, and blow out all cares, concerns, and worries that you may have collected during the day. Continuing to breathe in and out very deeply, begin to go within.

As you turn your attention inward, you may notice a dim light deep within you. Look within until you start to see just a bit of light, as if it is shining through dark clouds. Ask those clouds to move away, like an airplane diving through the clouds until you reach the light within you. Focus inside, and surround yourself with this white light of pure energy that will comfort you throughout the evening.

Take a moment to enjoy the safety and comfort of sinking in and falling into this white light, allowing it to hold you gently like a white cloud. So comfortable, so safe and serene. You know that you are completely loved, completely taken care of, and you enjoy this feeling of letting go.

As you think about your day today, be willing to forgive anyone who may have triggered any irritation, fear, anger, or other negative responses. Mentally tell that person, "I forgive you. I release you. I forgive you completely. I release you. I am free, and you are free."

Think about anyone else who may have triggered negative reactions in you, and release and forgive each person one by one. You are giving yourself the gift of complete freedom from all negativity, because you know that the price of resentment is too expensive. You simply choose to release all negative feelings, without judging yourself in any way for holding in these feelings. Instead, release them just as you would cleanse any soil off of your face or your body.

Release any anger you may be holding. Release any fear, putting it on the shelf for the evening, knowing that love is the true power within you, and love is the opposite of fear. Release any anxiety or worry, just letting it go as if it were a piece of paper that you were setting down. Know that as you clear your consciousness, there is no need to worry or be concerned. You release all tendencies to make plans, because for the evening, you free your mind from its shackles. Rejoice in this freedom of being completely untethered and completely cleansed.

Search your heart, mind, and body for any remaining negativity, and if you find any, just release it. Release it from your body, from your mind, and from your heart. Fill your heart with warm feelings of love, love for all of humanity, and for every situation that you go through. Know that every experience is for your soul growth and for your learning and teaching. Give thanks for all the lessons encountered during the day. Release all tendencies to *judge people or situations, knowing that judgments lower vibrations from the level of love and cloud you in a blanket of fear. Since you choose to stay at the high vibration and frequency of love, it's an easy decision to simply release all negative feelings now.*

Give gratitude for the day, and know that you are creating the life of your dreams. No matter how little progress appears to be occurring, it all adds up in the same positive direction. Give thanks as you recall the strangers and loved ones who entered your life today and who asked, "May I help you?"

Give thanks for the situations that appear to be coincidences, knowing that you attracted these situations into your consciousness and experience. Be grateful for coincidences, knowing that tomorrow you will attract even more. You do attract miracles into your life! It's so wonderful to be aware of the miracle that you are! You have so much to give, so much to do to help the world. You are allowing yourself to realize your true state of happiness, complete peace, and bliss.

As you continue to release anything negative within your core, your body, and mind, relax and get ready for a wonderful night of sleep. Sleep like a baby, so peaceful, so sweet. Sleep that is filled with wondrous, beautiful dreams that you easily remember at will. If you have a question for your inner guide or a request for something to occur, ask it right now. Know that throughout the night you will be given answers, guidance, and solutions. You will remember these answers when you awaken in the morning. If you choose, you can write them down so that you will remember them and have access to this information throughout the day.

As you slowly drift off into your evening slumber, you feel so grateful for so many people in your life. Counting your blessings is an ancient means of going off to sleep, and you claim the wisdom of this ancient tradition today by counting your blessings of people for whom you are grateful. Know that this gratitude also heals and strengthens all your relationships.

And as your heart and spirit is now cleansed and filled with gifts of love, I bid you, "Good night and sweet dreams."

Points to Remember

🐦 Meditation is more dependent upon quality time than quantity time.

🐦 We can access advice and information through meditation.

🐦 There is no right or wrong way to meditate; however, it helps to try different approaches and see which fits most comfortably into your lifestyle.

🐦 🐦 🐦

SWEET DREAMS

"I have never begun any important venture for which I felt adequately prepared."

— DR. SHELDON KOPP, AUTHOR OF
RAISE YOUR RIGHT HAND AGAINST FEAR

Getting a grip on time is like grabbing a handful of clouds—it vanishes the minute you think you've got it. Still, there are many ways to conquer time anxieties and gain control over interruptions that bleed your schedule and energy levels. We've talked about many down-to-earth and unearthly ways to manage your day. Still, the final decision about how to spend the moments of your day, year, and life rests in your own hands.

If you're tired of feeling like a time pauper, then vow to stick to these healthy promises to yourself:

MY VOWS: IT'S TIME TO BE GOOD TO MYSELF

1. "I vow to remain peaceful and take plenty of deep breaths in all circumstances."
2. "I allow my mind to stay calm and reasonable about time."
3. "I affirm, 'I have an abundance of time,' and 'My life is perfectly ordered right now.'"

4. "I know that I have the right to stick to my priorities. I do not allow interruptions and intrusions to veer me off my course."
5. "I affirm that my schedule has plenty of breathing room and allows me time to enjoy alone and with my family."
6. "I now plan ahead and give myself enough time so that I don't have to rush or worry about arriving late."
7. "I easily say 'no' to inappropriate requests for my time."
8. "I always consult and obey my intuition."
9. "I let go of concerns and fears about money, knowing that my only concern is to fulfill my divine assignment. I know that as long as I stay on path, all my material needs will be miraculously supplied."
10. "I laugh, have fun, and delight in the dreams I have built during this lifetime."

You Can Do It!

Changing your schedule and sticking to your priorities may make you feel like a newborn colt initially—wobbly, fragile, and off-balance. It can take 30 or 40 days to replace an old habit with a new one. With each mini-success and triumph, though, your new schedule will self-reinforce into a solid and stable lifestyle.

Reward yourself along the way, and enjoy your newfound leisure time with your friends and family. If something doesn't work in your life or makes you unhappy, take immediate action! Nobody knows how you feel but you, and you have the right to change your life—right now!

There will never be a more perfect time than today to carve out the life that makes you and your loved ones happy. It's a mistake to wait for some far-off future day when you'll have more time, money, have lost the excess weight, or have better conditions. It's an even bigger mistake to give away control of your time while awaiting permission to relax or make changes. If you feel stuck in a perpetual procrastination rut, ask yourself, *"What am I waiting for?"*

You can change your life,
and *you* do have the time!

I wish you many enjoyable, relaxing,
and healthful hours for years to come!

ॐ ॐ ॐ

Appendix

B I B L I O G R A P H Y

Association for Research and Enlightenment (1989) *Edgar Cayce on Channeling Your Higher Self,* by Henry Reed, Charles Thomas Cayce (Ed.). New York: Warner Books.

The Bible, New King James Version and Revised Standard Version.

Barash, Marc Ian (July 1994) The Amazing Power of Visualization. *Natural Health Magazine.*

Benner, Joseph S. (1991) *The Impersonal Life* (originally published in 1941). Marina del Rey, CA: DeVorss & Co.

Blavatsky, Helena Petrovna (1992) *The Voice of the Silence* (originally published in 1889). Wheaton, IL: The Theosophical Publishing House.

Bristol, Claude M. (1948) *The Magic of Believing.* New York: Cornerstone Library.

Dobrzynski, J. H. Should I have left an hour earlier? *The New York Times,* June 18, 1995, III, 1:4.

Ehrenreich, B. In search of a simpler life. *Working Woman,* December 1995, p. 27 (4).

Eddy, Mary Baker. (1971) *Science and Health with Key to the Scriptures* (originally published in 1875). Boston: The First Church of Christ, Scientist.

Emerson, Ralph Waldo (Ziff, L., Ed., 1982) *Selected Essays.* New York: Viking Penguin.

Foundation for Inner Peace (1975) *A Course in Miracles.* Glen Ellen, CA.

_____ (1976) *Psychotherapy: Purpose, Process and Practice.* Glen Ellen, CA.

Fox, Emmet. *The Mental Equivalent: The Secret of Demonstration* Unity Village, MO: Unity School of Christianity.

_____ (1934) *The Sermon on the Mount.* New York: Grosset & Dunlap.

Goldberg, C. Choosing the joys of a simplified life. *The New York Times,* Sept. 21, 1995, C1 (2).

Hay, Louise L. (1995) *Life! Reflections on Your Journey.* Carlsbad, CA: Hay House.

Holmes, Ernest (1984) *Living the Science of Mind.* Marina del Rey, CA: DeVorss & Co.

_____ (1988) *The Science of Mind: Fiftieth Anniversary Edition.* New York: G. P. Putnam's Sons.

Leisure Intelligence. Trends in leisure time. Summer 1995, *v. 2,* p. 1 (7).

Marks, J. Time out. *U.S. News & World Report,* Dec. 11, 1995, v. 119, p. 4 (8).

Merrill, S.D. Wanna do my weekend shopping? *U.S. News & World Report,* April 24, 1989, *v. 113,* p. 80 (1).

Murphy, Joseph (1965) *The Amazing Laws of Cosmic Mind Power.* West Nyack, NY.: Parker Publisher Co.

_____ (1966) *Your Infinite Power to Be Rich.* West Nyack, NY: Parker Publishing Co.

Owen, K. Who's watching the kids? *The Los Angeles Times,* Feb. 20, 1995, A, 5:2.

Ponder, Catherine (1987) *The Millionaires of Genesis.* Marina del Rey, CA: DeVorss & Co.

_____ (1985) *The Dynamic Laws of Prosperity.* Marina del Rey, CA: DeVorss & Co.

Price, John Randolph (1987, 1996) *The Abundance Book.* Carlsbad, CA: Hay House.

_____ (1981) *The Superbeings.* New York: Ballantine Books.

Robinson, J. P. Your money, your life. *American Demographics,* Nov. 1991, *v. 13,* p. 22 (3).

Russell, C. Overworked? Overwhelmed? *American Demographics,* March 1995, *v. 17,* p. 8 (2).

Samuels, Mike and Nancy (1975) *Seeing With the Mind's Eye: The History, Techniques and Uses of Visualization.* New York: Random House.

Spring, J. Exercising the brain. *American Demographics*, Oct. 1993, *v. 15*, p. 5 (4).

_____ Seven days of play. *American Demographics*, March 1993, *v. 15*, p. 50 (4).

Wilde, Stuart (1989) *The Trick to Money Is Having Some*. Carlsbad, CA: Hay House.

Williams, Andrew, Ed. (1991) *World Scripture: A Comparative Anthology of Sacred Texts, a Project of the International Religious Foundation*. New York: Paragon House.

Yogananda, Paramahansa (1944) *The Law of Success*. Los Angeles: International Publications Council of Self-Realization Fellowship.

_____ (1988) *Where There Is Light*. Los Angeles: International Publications Council of Self-Realization Fellowship.

The following list of resources can be used for more information about recovery options for issues surrounding addictions, health concerns, death and bereavement, or problems related to dysfunctional families. The addresses and telephone numbers listed are for the national headquarters; look in your local yellow pages under "Community Services" for resources closer to your area.

In addition to the following groups, other self-help organizations may be available in your area to assist your healing and recovery for a particular life crisis not listed here. Consult your telephone directory, call a counseling center or help line near you, or write or call:

American Self-Help Clearinghouse
St. Clares-Riverside Medical Center
Denville, NJ 07834
(201) 625-7101

National Self-Help Clearinghouse
25 West 43rd St., Room 620
New York, NY 10036
(212) 642-2944

AIDS
_____

AIDS Hotline
(800) 342-2437

Children with AIDS Project of America
4020 N. 20th St., Ste. 101
Phoenix, AZ 85016
(602) 265-4859
Hotline
(602) 843-8654

The Names Project— AIDS Quilt
(800) 872-6263

National AIDS Network
(800) 342-2437

National Association for People with AIDS
2025 "I" St. NW, Ste. 1101
Washington, DC 20006
(202) 429-2856

Project Inform
19655 Market St., Ste. 220
San Francisco, CA 94103
(415) 558-8669

PWA Coalition
50 W. 17th St.
New York, NY 10011

Spanish AIDS Hotline
(800) 344-7432

TDD (Hearing Impaired) AIDS Hotline
(800) 243-7889

ALCOHOL ABUSE

Al-Anon Family Headquarters
200 Park Ave. South
New York, NY 10003
(212) 302-7240

Alcoholics Anonymous (AA)
General Service Office
475 Riverside Dr.
New York, NY 10115
(212) 870-3400

Children of Alcoholics Foundation
P.O. Box 4185
Grand Central Station
New York, NY 10163-4185
(212) 754-0656
(800) 359-COAF

Meridian Council, Inc.
Administrative Offices
4 Elmcrest Terrace
Norwalk, CT 06850

National Association of Children of Alcoholics (NACOA)
11426 Rockville Pike, Ste. 100
Rockville, MD 20852
(301) 468-0985

National Clearinghouse for Alcohol and Drug Information (NCADI)
P.O. Box 234
Rockville, MD 20852
(301) 468-2600

National Council on Alcoholism and Drug Dependency (NCADD)
12 West 21st St.
New York, NY 10010
(212) 206-6770

ANOREXIA/BULIMIA

American Anorexia/Bulimia Association, Inc.
293 Central Park West, Ste. 1R
New York, NY 10024
(212) 501-8351
(212) 501-0342

Bulimic/Anorexic Self-Help (BASH)
P.O. Box 39903
St. Louis, MO 63138
(800) 888-4680

Eating Disorder Organization
1925 East Dublin Granville Rd.
Columbus, OH 43229-3517
(614) 436-1112

CANCER

National Cancer Institute
(800) 4-CANCER

Commonweal
P.O. Box 316
Bolinas, CA 94924
(415) 868-0971

ECAP
(Exceptional Cancer Patients)
Bernie S. Siegel, M.D.
300 Plaza Middlesex
Middletown, CT 06457
(800) 700-8869

CHILDREN'S ISSUES

CHILD MOLESTATION

Adults Molested As Children
United (AMACU)
232 East Gish Rd.
San Jose, CA 95112
(800) 422-4453

National Committee for
Prevention of Child Abuse
322 South Michigan Ave.,
Ste. 1600
Chicago, IL 60604
(312) 663-3520

CHILDREN'S AND TEENS' CRISIS INTERVENTION

Boy's Town Crisis Hotline
(800) 448-3000

Covenant House Hotline
(800) 999-9999

Kid Save
(800) 543-7283

National Runaway
and Suicide Hotline
(800) 621-4000

MISSING CHILDREN

Childsearch
Six Beacon St.
Boston, MA 02108
(617) 720-1760

Missing Children-Help Center
410 Ware Blvd., Ste. 400
Tampa, FL 33619
(800) USA-KIDS

National Center for Missing
and Exploited Children
1835 K St. NW
Washington, DC 20006
(800) 843-5678

TERMINALLY ILL CHILDREN (FULFILLING WISHES)

Brass Ring Society
7020 S. Yale Ave., Ste. 103
Tulsa, OK 74136
(918) 496-2838

The Candlelighters Childhood
Cancer Foundation
1901 Pennsylvania Ave. NW
Ste. 1001
Washington, DC 20006
(202) 659-5136

A Wish with Wings
P.O. Box 110418
Arlington, TX 76007
(817) 261-8752

CO-DEPENDENCY

Co-Dependents Anonymous
P.O. Box 33577
Phoenix, AZ 85067-3577
(602) 277-7991

DEATH/GRIEVING/ SUICIDE

American Association of Suicidology
2459 South Ash St.
Denver, CO 80222
(303) 692-0985

Concern for Dying
250 W. 57th St.
New York, NY 10107
(212) 246-6962

Elisabeth Kubler-Ross Center
South Route 616
Head Waters, VA 24442
(703) 396-3441

Forum for Death Education and Counsel (FDEC)
2211 Arthur Ave.
Lakewood, OH 44107
(216) 228-0334

Grief Recovery Helpline
(800) 445-4808

Grief Recovery Institute
8306 Wilshire Blvd., Ste. 21A
Beverly Hills, CA 90211
(213) 650-1234

Mothers Against Drunk Driving (MADD)
669 Airport Freeway, Ste. 310
Hurst, TX 76053
(817) 268-6233

National Hospice Organization (NHO)
1901 N. Ft. Myer Dr., Ste. 402
Arlington, VA 22209
(703) 243-5900

National Sudden Infant Death Syndrome
Two Metro Plaza, Ste. 205
Landover, MD 20785
(800) 221-SIDS

Parents of Suicides
15 E. Brinkerhoff Ave.
Palisades Park, NJ 07650
(201) 585-7608

Seasons: Suicide Bereavement
4777 Naniola Dr.
Salt Lake City, UT 84117

Widowed Persons Service
1909 K St., NW
Washington, DC 20049
(202) 872-4700

DEBTS

Debtors Anonymous
General Service Office
P.O. Box 400
Grand Central Station
New York, NY 10163-0400
(212) 642-8220

DIABETES

American Diabetes Association
(800) 232-3472

DRUG ABUSE

Cocaine Anonymous
(800) 347-8998

National Cocaine-Abuse Hotline
(800) 262-2463
(800) COCAINE

National Institute of Drug Abuse (NIDA)
Parklawn Building
5600 Fishers Lane, Room 10A-39
Rockville, MD 20852
(301) 443-6245 (for information)
(800) 662-4357 (for help)

World Service Office (NA)
P.O. Box 9999
Van Nuys, CA 91409
(818) 780-3951

EATING DISORDERS

Food Addiction Hotline
Florida Institute of Technology
FIT Hotline
Drug Addiction & Depression
(800) 872-0088

Overeaters Anonymous
National Office
Rio Rancho, NM
(505) 891-2664

GAMBLING

Gamblers Anonymous
National Council on Compulsive Gambling
444 West 59th St., Room 1521
New York, NY 10019
(212) 265-8600

HEALTH ISSUES

Alzheimer's Disease Information
(800) 621-0379

American Chronic Pain Association
P.O. Box 850
Rocklin, CA 95677
(916) 632-0922

American Foundation of Traditional Chinese Medicine
1280 Columbus Ave., Ste. 302
San Francisco, CA 94133
(415) 776-0502

American Holistic Health Association
P.O. Box 17400
Anaheim, CA 92817
(714) 779-6152

Center for Human Potential and Mind-Body Medicine
Deepak Chopra, M.D.
973 B Lomas Santa Fe Dr.
Solana Beach, CA 92075
(619) 794-2425

The Fetzer Institute
9292 West KL Ave.
Kalamazoo, MI 49009
(616) 375-2000

Hippocrates Health Institute
1443 Palmdale Court
West Palm Beach, FL 33411
(407) 471-8876

Hospicelink
(800) 331-1620

Institute for Noetic Sciences
P.O. Box 909, Dept. M
Sausalito, CA 94966-0909
(800) 383-1394

241

The Mind-Body Medical Institute
185 Pilgrim Rd.
Boston, MA 02215
(617) 732-7000

National Health Information Center
P.O. Box 1133
Washington, DC 20013-1133
(800) 336-4797

Optimum Health Care Institute
6970 Central Ave.
Lemon Grove, CA 91945
(619) 464-3346

Preventive Medicine Institute
Dean Ornish, M.D.
900 Bridgeway, Ste. 2
Sausalito, CA 94965
(415) 332-2525

World Research Foundation
15300 Ventura Blvd., Ste. 405
Sherman Oaks, CA 91403
(818) 907-5483

IMPOTENCE

Impotency Institute of America
2020 Pennsylvania Ave. N.W.,
Ste. 292
Washington, DC 20006
(800) 669-1603

INCEST

Incest Survivors Resource Network International, Inc.
P.O. Box 7375
Las Cruces, NM 88006-7375
(505) 521-4260

COURSE IN MIRACLES COUNSELORS

Miracle Distribution Center
1141 East Ash Avenue
Fullerton, CA 92631
(714) 738-8380
(Call or write for a list of therapists in your area)

PET BEREAVEMENT

Bide-A-Wee Foundation
New York, NY
(212) 532-6395

The Animal Medical Center
New York, NY
(212) 838-8100

Holistic Animal Consulting Center
Staten Island, NY
(718) 720-5548

RAPE

Austin Rape Crisis Center
1824 East Oltorf
Austin, TX 78741
(512) 440-7273

SEX ADDICTIONS

National Council on Sexual Addictions
P.O. Box 652
Azle, TX 76098-0652
(800) 321-2066

SMOKING ABUSE

Nicotine Anonymous
2118 Greenwich St.
San Francisco, CA 94123
(415) 750-0328

SPOUSAL ABUSE

National Coalition Against Domestic Violence
P.O. Box 34103
Washington, DC 20043-4103
(202) 638-6388
(800) 333-7233 (crisis line)

National Domestic Violence Hotline
(800) 799-SAFE

STRESS REDUCTION

The Biofeedback & Psychophysiology Clinic
The Menninger Clinic
P.O. Box 829
Topeka, KS 66601-0829
(913) 273-7500

New York Open Center
(In-depth workshops to invigorate the spirit)
83 Spring St.
New York, NY 10012
(212) 219-2527

Omega Institute
(A healing, spiritual retreat community)
260 Lake Dr.
Rhinebeck, NY 12572-3212
(914) 266-4444 (info)
(800) 944-1001 (to enroll)

Rise Institute
P.O. Box 2733
Petaluma, CA 94973
(707) 765-2758

The Stress Reduction Clinic
Jon Kabat-Zinn, Ph.D.
University of Massachusetts
Medical Center
55 Lake Avenue North
Worcester, MA 01655
(508) 856-1616

Index

lack mentality, 2, 17-18
Lansky, V., 91-92
Leisure Intelligence Journal, x
lethargy, 61
love life, 147-167
  manifesting, 49-51, 159-163, 197,
    202-203
manifesting, 20-28, 106-107
martyr/victim roles, 72-73
meaningless meetings, 123
meditation, 190, 215-233
  to contact inner guide, 220-222
Meir, G., 85
Merck poll, x
money, xii-xiii, 33, 169-171, 204-205,
  207-208
morning meditation, 219-220
negativity
  releasing, 16-18, 81-82, 85-99, 115,
    207-208, 227-229, 232
  self-talk, 73
Novaco, R., 179-180
outlining, 210-211
overeating, iii, 15, 61, 124
Paracelsus, 200
parenting, 151, 182
physical illness, 61, 79-81
Ponder, C., 171
Price, J. R., 171
Price, M. L., 47
priorities
  identifying, 9, 103-105, 109, 123
  national surveys, ix-xiii
  sticking to, 111-112, 231-233
procrastination, 7-8, 59-83, 136-137
procrastination pals, 121-126
psychic abilities, 189-191, 208-209
qualities of happy successful people,
  109-110
quiz, time crunch, xi
rationalizing, 76
relationships
  manifesting love, 49-51, 159-163,
    197, 202-203
  problematic, 61-62, 73, 163-166
  romantic, 148-151, 159-163
  spiritual healing of, 163-166
  with children, 85-87, 151-158, 182
  with family, 85-87, 151-158

Rodriguez, M. 89-91
Roper polls, x
safety cage, 93-94
saying, "no," 125, 232
self-care, 156, 158-159, 231-233
self-fulfilling fears, 78-79
self-permission, 77-78, 94-98
self-responsibility, 96-97
self-sabotage, 71-75
simplicity, x-xi
spare time, x, 2-3
spirit guides, 21-28, 120, 187-195,
  220-222
spiritual healing of relationships, 163-
  166
spiritual path, 29-30, 193-195
spiritual powers, 3
spiritual protection, 118-119
sport fighting, 122-123
steps to accomplishment, 130-131
stress, x, 112-113
  and commuting, 179-182
surrender, 191-192
television viewing, 4-6, 124-125, 152
think and grow rich theories, 31
time crunch, xi-xii
time inventory, 105-106
time management, 103-126, 176-179
time wasters, 117-127
U.S. News & World Report/Bozell
  survey, x, xiii
visualization
  guidelines, 197-198, 201-203
  history of, 199-201
waiting for permission, 77-78, 94-98
Walter, D., 85-87
weekend time management, 6
Wharton School study, xii-xiii
Wilde, S., 171
Wilson, W., 197
Winfrey, O., 98-99
worry, 126
Yogananda, P., 13, 215, 216
Yoruba Proverbs, 204

245

N O T E S

ABOUT THE AUTHOR

Doreen Virtue, Ph.D., is a fourth-generation metaphysician who maintains a counseling practice specializing in identifying and manifesting true purpose and desire. She is the bestselling author of *Losing Your Pounds of Pain* and *Constant Craving*. Dr. Virtue frequently appears on radio and television, including *Oprah, Sally, Leeza, Montel,* and *CNN.* She is a contributing editor and advice columnist for *Complete Woman* magazine, and a frequent contributor to *Woman's World* magazine.

Dr. Virtue welcomes your letters and personally answers all correspondence. Please write to her c/o Hay House, Inc., P.O. Box 5100, Carlsbad, CA 92018-5100. Please call the Publicity Director at Hay House: (800) 654-5126, to inquire about arranging or attending a workshop with Dr. Virtue.